MEMOMAN'S MESSAGE TO THE UNIVERSE

By Luke Soiseth
September, 2017

ISBN: 978-0-692-93148-6

Cover photograph by Darin Back Photography
Book design by MOD, www.modandco.com

www.memoman.me

Printed by CreateSpace, An Amazon.com Company
Printed in Charleston, SC

St. Paul, Minnesota

For Jana, for everything; Olivia and Benjamin; my mother, Cherrol Bloom Soiseth; and in memory of my father, Robert Perry Soiseth.

INTRODUCTION

My name is not actually Memoman in so far as that's not what my mom calls me, but this message is his and he's only sort of me. A while back I recorded a video called "Memoman's Message to the Millennials," in which I asked that they drop the whole Millennials moniker and become the Meditation Generation instead (I coined the term myself and hoped it would stick). I argued rightfully that the world is a fucking mess in a lot of ways and if Millennials worldwide did this one simple thing – meditation – and taught their children to do the same, the world would be an infinitely better place, which is still true.

I uploaded the video to YouTube and pretty much no one watched it.

About a month after making the video I had The Experience (that's what I call it), and it totally freaked me out. These sorts of things don't happen to guys like me, and so I needed to figure out what happened and why. I did some research. I kept on meditating, introspecting, and exploring my own mind, as I've learned to do. And I looked to the past, and particularly the preceding year, for things that might be complicit in The Experience. It was an interesting year.

My father had died at the end of May after a brutal final year on this planet. I was still drinking good and hard, which was adding fuel to my usual anxiety and depression. When autumn hit, I hit rock bottom and ended up at the doctor, then on an anti-depressant and then, within another month, I suddenly quit drinking. I saw a psychologist. I got deep into my meditation practice again, as well as my running. I got a ukulele. I lost 35 pounds.

And so now I've basically rewritten my plea for Millennial meditation in light of The Experience and all it has kicked up in my life. Memoman's Message to the Universe is about memory and the mind; it's about music and movies, truth and opinion, desire, craving, empathy, knowledge, science, nature, wonder and drugs; it's about religion and spirituality; it is still a plea for us all to meditate and/or find other ways to understand (and own) our own minds, our unconscious, our biases and belief systems, and to embrace our profound uniqueness, our many similarities, and our mind-blowing good fortune at just being here – with unfathomably brilliant and complex brains – on this tiny brilliant dot in a giant Universe.

I've also expanded my audience to include the entire Universe. Go hard or go home.

THE EXPERIENCE — THIS REALLY HAPPENED

I sit down to meditate on the night of January 30, 2015, as I had every other night before bed since I quit drinking, which was on November 30, 2014. I had meditated for about a decade off and on, but only now had my practice really taken off due to actually practicing and, no doubt, because I had quit drinking. My meditations were deeper, longer and more interesting. The benefits came quickly.

So I was happy; really happy, in fact. My family and I were healthy and loving; we had a little home and a dog, lots of debt and no real savings, but corking the booze, going onto a psychotropic medication and practicing my meditation had done wonders for my anxiety and depression. Even the bad days were not so bad, and certainly not from a worldly perspective. I was no longer lying awake in the wee hours of the morning worrying about money or the end of the world or anything else. In fact, I had it quite good and I knew it. And I know it now. I am truly blessed.

Earlier in the evening, I had played the ukulele received on my birthday two months before – November 26, 2014, since we're talking dates. I had played the ukulele really well – like really, really well – far beyond what I would say I was capable of. I'm the first to admit that I'm not all that proficient on the thing (even now), yet I was winging around the frets, nailing every note and chord. I was certain a muse hovered over my chair, bestowing upon me this sudden talent I otherwise did not possess.

So I begin my meditation in really good spirits, ready to cruise the brain fantastic, as nobody says. I settle into myself, seated half-lotus, pillow under butt, ambient music playing softly in my ears. I close my eyes, relax my body, feel the pull of gravity, the weight and density of my corporeal self, and focus solely and patiently on my breathing. I count my breaths:

Breathe In/Out One, In/Out Two, In/Out Three...

Man, I was playing that thing well! I suddenly think. That was sweet. It's a really good ukulele, or I think it is. What do I know? I only have one ukulele so I'm not exactly an expert on the quality of a particular ukulele, but, wow, that furnace is really loud, when was the last time I changed the filter? I remember the filters in True cigarettes, like little pie charts.

I think about my first cigarette under a weeping willow by a lake and how much I hated it and yet at some point I was smoking every day. Why is that? It tasted like shit and yet it became a habit, and thank goodness, I quit, well, mostly I quit. I can't really say I quit completely because drinking leads to smoking for me. That's your gateway drug right there – drinking. And now that I'm not drinking I guess I'm much less likely to...

My mind babbles on and on, which is exactly how our minds sound if we pay any attention to them. The stream of consciousness flows continuously, and quieting the mind, and especially the ever-distracted modern mind, is extremely difficult. Hence the meditation.

I shake it off, refocus on my breathing, and begin again at one.

Breathe In/Out One, In/Out Two, In/Out Three…

God, I don't want to go to that stupid meeting tomorrow. I'm not even remotely ready!

Breathe In/Out One… I should skip it and just stay home!

Breathe In/Out One… I would love a day off.

Breathe In/Out One… There's no coffee at the office.

On and on it goes: Me trying to focus my mind and settle into a lovely meditation and my mind having other ideas, complaints, queries, wishes, realizations, and random outbursts. Still, though, this is pretty much par for the course, so I keep on trying.

Then something changes. It's like the pitch shifts darker — a muddier stream of consciousness. First it is just anxiety, a flutter in my chest for no apparent reason, but then disturbing thoughts, images and memories start popping into my mind. None of them become complete thoughts, but just the awareness of them brings on some of their effects. I try to keep focus, recognize the thoughts, and, as I was taught, allow them to pass through my consciousness like clouds through a clear blue sky.

It doesn't work.

Breathe In/Out One, In/Out Two. Damn it! That meeting is important and I'm totally not fucking ready.

Relax.

Breathe In/Out One… Tom would love seeing us fuck this thing up. He's such an asshole! I'm so sick of work!

Breathe In/Out One… And now I've got to deal with Olivia's sleepover! What if the kid's dad is some fucking pervert?

I actually laugh at that, but it isn't funny. It feels like a foregone conclusion.

Oh, for God's sake! I sit down to meditate and now I'm actually pissed off? This is just perfect!

I really am pissed off. I was genuinely looking forward to my meditation, and pissed off is generally not one of the expected outcomes of a healthy meditation practice.

We're so screwed tomorrow. Why the fuck didn't I prepare just a tiny little bit, for God's sake! What a dumbass! Tom's such a dick! I don't even fucking care…

Honestly, I have these sorts of thoughts on occasion. Most of us do, and it's certainly not the strangest thing our brains are capable of. But my meditation practice had calmed me down quite a bit and kept me on a much more even keel overall. The usual histrionics I was perfectly capable of, related to just about anything at any time, seemed to be mostly history. So while I am a little taken aback by my attitude at this moment,

I don't feel like I am losing touch with reality quite yet.

Fuck it. *I give in. It's hopeless. The angry shit just keeps coming, and while I could sit and watch it – clouds through a clear blue sky and all of that – this I don't want to watch at all.*

I get up and head for the stairs. I have a strange and very tangible sensation that the malevolent thoughts are following me – physically – and are right at my heels. I think about ghosts and jump the last three steps into the kitchen.

The house shakes with a passing train so I know it's heavy and probably loaded with fracking oil – big black missiles filled with dirty explosive shit, speeding by at easily 40 miles per hour, three houses away and in the fucking dark! What a bunch of greedy bastards!

Every clack, clang and shudder the train makes as it snakes its way past our house rattles my bones. I remember the letter we received from the State regarding the trains and the fracking oil: Our house is in a blast zone! Who lives in a fucking blast zone!?

I imagine the train as it jumps the tracks and the cars buckle, metal crashes into metal, oil splashes out, sparks fly and the cul de sac explodes in a shower of fracked fucking napalm and jagged iron rockets smash through the four-plex down the street, the neighbors' house, and then ours.

We'll go in the basement!

What?! 'We'll go in the basement'? Perfect! We can just burn together under the stairs then, dumbass!

I take out a yogurt in the kitchen, open it and have one bite. I can't eat it, but it's not just that I can't eat it. The very fact that I can't eat the yogurt fills me with enormous anxiety. I should eat it. I'll throw it out, or is it recyclable? I don't know. Fuck! What do I do? *The question overwhelms me. It's like having to decide between killing one brother or another — recyclable or not. It's ludicrous. I know it is. But it's huge right now — overwhelming. I drop the yogurt into the sink and head up the next flight of stairs to the second floor. This time the ghosts chase me up, I swear to God, and I look behind me certain to see red-eyed spirits swirling around the staircase, laughing, leering, and lunging at me.*

I slip into the bedroom I share with my wife. She lies beneath the quilts. "I think I'm going crazy," I say. She doesn't move. I say it again and she sleeps on. She makes such a small bump beneath the covers and I feel profound dread — for her, the kids and myself. We are so vulnerable! *The train jumps the tracks and explodes again and I flinch.*

I turn around and cross the hallway to the bathroom, the old wood floors cracking beneath my feet. I feel for the switch, flip on the light, and…

…*I SEE GOD*.

[To be continued…]

WHO AM I? [THE SON OF MY FATHER]

I'm the guy who needs to stop and say that I'm agnostic in these God matters. I always have been. Even in Sunday School, I could never make that leap from the usual lessons of good behavior to walking on water. I thought it was a cool idea, no doubt, but always assumed it was all made up, and conveniently, 2,000 years ago. It might be genetic and it might be a learned belief, and it might be both, but I was a Sunday School skeptic from an early age and I still am.

It makes some sense. My dad was a doctor – a scientist – and so he respected the sort of truth that is proven or provable and while he came from a long line of serious Lutherans, he wasn't going to spend much time engaged in it himself.

When I was younger, he never said that outright, but it had to be a wedding or a funeral for Dad to cross that holy threshold, and maybe all that rubbed off on me. Either way, when I heard people say things like, "I See God," I always had the same reaction: "You're full of shit."

After he retired, he told me a bit more. He said that he was never able to square a supposedly just and loving god with the eight-year-old girl whose body was crushed by a drunk driver and which he had to piece back together in the middle of the night. And the loved ones would pray and beseech their god and the girl may or may not ever walk again, she may or may not even live. How could he believe prayer worked when he saw it fail constantly. And if he were to believe it worked, what then of when it didn't, when the innocent child died on the table? What was this God thinking then? Dad had no patience for "mysterious ways."

I grew to agree with all of that.

But now this? What was God doing here at my house? I didn't sign up for a religious experience. I'm not even a religious guy. Nor was I crouching in a foxhole or hanging from a cliff. I was sitting on a cushion, minding my own mind.

A MIND FOR DRINKING

Prior to The Experience, I was drinking like a madman and had been for a good 25 years. I don't know if I drank any more in the months after my father died, but that would have been difficult to do. If anything, I was devoted. I drank every day – rain, sleet, snow, flu – it didn't matter, and I started young. I wrapped my mom and dad's Buick around a telephone pole drunk one night in high school. It was stupid beyond belief. I had two friends in the car and thankfully neither one was hurt but for a chipped tooth. We ran back to my chipped-tooth friend's house and the shit ensued. You'd think that would teach a guy, but fast-forward 30 years and I was still at it – but for the driving drunk.

So, I did the math. I averaged nine beers a night for two decades. Nine beers x 365 days x 20 years = 65,700 cold ones. I did not skip nights, even when I was sick (brandy does wonders) and 20 years is on the low side as I could have probably more accurately inserted 25 years. Sixty-five thousand beers. Allow that to blow your mind. It certainly blew mine.

In hindsight, I can see that it took an amazing amount of control over my mind. There was no question that I would begin drinking at my earliest convenience after work, and I worked to make that happen fast. Then I would drink until I went to bed. To stop drinking while remaining awake for any length of time was awful, nearly impossible and to be avoided at all costs.

I occasionally went out drinking, but would generally rather stay home. Then I didn't have to drive, pay a cab or get a ride, and being home allowed me to drink with abandon and the peace of mind that I always knew where the next drink was coming from. I would not "get caught" because I had built up a wicked tolerance so it was never very apparent that I was hammered.

Drinking like that is a learned behavior. My brain – my conscious and unconscious minds (in cahoots) – got really, really practiced at getting booze and getting drunk. Just like learning to play an instrument, the practice – the repetition – trained the brain to stay on the right track to achieving drunkenness. That's how I got so good at it.

I was always prepared. I planned ahead, counted my beers, stacked the recycling just right, pushed the little airplane vodka bottles down into the bottom of the trash, and always knew where the next drink was coming from. Nobody needed to know that for every drink they saw me have, there was another one they didn't. And God bless television, the great distractor. I waited for a "good part" then went to make a really good pour for myself.

I may have remained in control of my drinking had I thought right out of the gate, say, right after I almost killed my friends, "You know, I might be prone to abusing this tasty liquid drug so I should probably be vigilant about my possible trajectory here." Instead, I was in a big cup on a giant catapult and ... Snip! Bang! Zoom! It was awesome!

Until it wasn't. I don't know when it happened but at some point, it was no longer all that awesome, but more of a burden. Instead of enjoying drinking I was obsessing about it – depressed at my own weakness in the face of it and filled with anxiety about my drinking, depression and everything else. I thought about drinking constantly, every day – it drained me; a long, slow one-sided emotional pummeling – and ultimately the 10,624 punches beat the shit out of me.

I'm not proud that I drank that much, but I'm happy that it didn't kill me. Or, put more honestly, that I didn't kill myself, or someone else. And I'm also no longer obsessing about it. The punches stopped and I'm happy as can be.

Please note that I was generally happy as can be drinking also. Most of it was great! And I'm certainly not looking for anyone's pity - I hardly suffered at all. All of this just seems like it might be relevant to why I had The Experience. Or not.

MINDLESS. POPCORN. CONSUMPTION.

I read about a study in which researchers chose 100 people to watch movie trailers and gave them each a box of popcorn. The popcorn was either fresh or 12 weeks old. Turns out the people who historically ate a lot of popcorn ate the same percentage of popcorn whether it was stale or fresh, while those who historically didn't eat much popcorn ate much less stale popcorn. It's like that. The power of the habit itself and not the joy of eating the popcorn – or drinking the beer – is what undergirds the mindless consumption.

I vowed to stop drinking many days only to, quite literally, find myself in the liquor store on the way home from work. Bam! I'm standing in front of the bright, cool, colorful coolers with an overwhelming selection to choose among. *But I wasn't going to come here,* I'd suddenly think.

Then: *Since I'm already here, I might as well grab a 12-pack and then quit tomorrow – for sure – instead.* And then since I had a 12-pack and I didn't want any beers around the next day to tempt me, I drank 11 instead of the usual nine that night, poured the last one out (but for a quick slug and a toast to future health) because, of course, I didn't want to drink a whole 12-pack.

Then I'd do it all over again.

"Questioning and naming our individual patterns are part of The Buddha's recipe for awakening from the sleep of illusion and delusion."[1]

— Lama Surya Das

UNDERSTANDING THE FOUR NOBLE TRUTHS

I found my way to Buddhism like a lot of people, attracted by the fact that it is less a religion than a philosophy that promotes a very selfless, thoughtful and peaceful way of living. There's no god at the center, but Siddhartha Gautama, The Buddha, who sometimes seems to be revered as one. The agnostic in me liked that because then I wouldn't be distracted by the god concept and could focus instead on the ideas, which are truly enlightening.

Two central Buddhist teachings are The Four Noble Truths and The Noble Eightfold Path. The latter was generally clear to me from the get-go and includes Right View, Right Thinking, Right Speech, Right Action, Right Livelihood, Right Diligence, Right Mindfulness, and Right Concentration. You can kind of get where those are going, but of course, there's much more to them and the reasoning and poetry they possess are worth looking at more closely.

The Four Noble Truths on the other hand didn't make sense to me. They are:

- Suffering;
- The origin, roots, nature, creation, or arising of suffering;
- The cessation of creating suffering by refraining from doing the things that make us suffer;
- And the path that leads to refraining from doing the things that cause us to suffer (aka The Noble Eightfold Path).[2]

It kind of bugged me that I didn't get it. I mean, I did, but it seemed so obvious: know there is suffering, figure out where the suffering comes from, stop doing it, then follow the Noble Eightfold Path and all's well. What was I missing? The Four Noble Truths are at the very center of Buddhism and I could not see how that could possibly mean more than how I understood it, but it must. So I mostly focused on The Noble Eightfold Path.

Then one day, not long after my Dad died, I was in my usual post-drunk funk, and I came across The Four Noble Truths again and suddenly it dawned on me.

It *is* that simple. I just have to apply it to my own life.

I know that might sound blatantly obvious to you, but it somehow never occurred to me. And for whatever reason, this simple idea in the form of the Four Noble Truths, that I'd read over and over, suddenly pierced my illusions.

I didn't stop drinking at that moment, but it made the path much clearer to me and I brought it to mind often as I continued to struggle with and obsess over my drinking. I was suffering, due to my drinking, I needed to stop my drinking, then get back to living a normal life. Huh. Who knew?

I'm not a Buddhist, or if I am, I'm not very good at it, and especially in regard to some parts of the Noble Eightfold Path (that may already be clear), but I got a gift from it – many gifts, in fact – and for that I'm thankful.

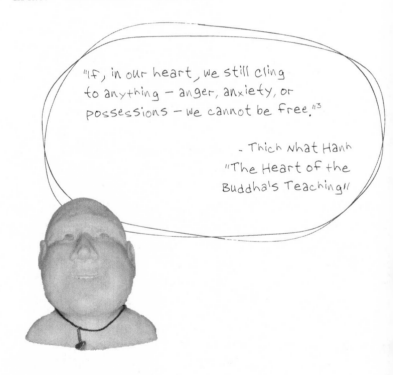

"If, in our heart, we still cling to anything — anger, anxiety, or possessions — we cannot be free."[3]

- Thich Nhat Hanh
"The Heart of the Buddha's Teaching"

DRINKS AND DOUGHNUTS

Alcohol is a great drug. It can make us happy, relaxed, ecstatic, eloquent, outgoing and provide us many other positive experiences. But there's a tipping point where all those positives recede and in comes stress, sadness, violence, lethargy, stupidity, depression, anxiety and more.

But I see now that, as powerful as alcohol is, I allowed it. Encouraged it even. I embraced it from the get-go. I never bothered to look at my drinking seriously, and I plowed over every red flag that popped up. I thought about drinking, talked about drinking, joked about drinking, planned for drinking, complained about drinking and surrendered to the cravings day after day, year after year, over and over and over again. That was me. I was entirely complicit. I'm the one who made certain it flourished but I wasn't the only one who suffered because of it.

How, pray tell, can a guy be surprised that he drank 65,700 beers?

It's like this: At some point, you become acquainted with doughnuts. You see them, taste them and enjoy them. A set of neurons fire in your brain and capture that: I like doughnuts. Then someone says to you, "I wish I had a doughnut," and some number of the same "doughnut neurons" that fired the first time, fire again, reminding you that you like doughnuts. It's not exact; the experience is not precisely the same, but there is a remembrance of pleasure that stokes desire.

Your ears perk up any time you hear something that sounds like doughnut. The smell entices you; even the packaging gets you a little hot and bothered. So you eat more doughnuts, and the repetition (want doughnut, eat doughnut) strengthens the connections and the doughnut neurons get even more ready and able to light up again.

Our brains create pleasure in the same manner whether it's booze, drugs or doughnuts. They do this by releasing a neurotransmitter called dopamine. Dopamine promotes desire. The more pleasurable something is to us, the more dopamine is released, and the more we've got to have it again. This is a blatant over-simplification of a very complex phenomenon, but basically true.

And the more we continue to satisfy the desire (to have a drink, do the drug, take a hit), the more focus our minds put to satisfying that desire again, repeating the process and learning the behavior to the point where we're single-minded in our pursuit of satisfying that one desire.

But of course, the pleasure lessens over time as our tolerance increases so we need more and more of whatever it is to feel the pleasure we once felt. So we increase the frequency and the amount to reach that original intensity until eventually we are simply no longer able to get there.

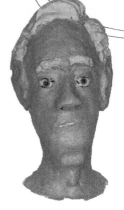

We can't get any higher. We no longer feel that wonderful pleasure. In fact, we (and the people who love us) are and have been suffering. That's addiction, as told by someone who is not a neuroscientist.

REPEAT AS DESIRED

In his book, "The Biology of Desire," Marc Lewis, a neuroscientist and professor of developmental psychology, argues that addiction should not be understood as a disease, but simply results "from the motivated repetition of the same thoughts and behaviors until they become habitual."[4] That repetition essentially changes the brain's wiring over time so that the goal of satisfying those desires eclipses all others.

You begin to not just like or want doughnuts, but really want doughnuts – need doughnuts –and your brain puts increasing emphasis on satisfying that one craving to where it can default to that behavior whether you like it or not. Your unconscious does an end-around of your consciousness and gets you to the liquor store while you're busy thinking about whatever else.

It's the repetition that changes the brain's wiring and not the doughnuts, the alcohol or cocaine. Repetition – anything we do over and over and over – is how we acquire habits, skills, knowledge, and addictions. Repetition is how we learn.

And repetition can be comforting. Habits are tiny rituals. They give our lives order and continuity. They make us feel good like coffee does every morning for many of us.

But craving is good, too, right? We crave many positive things. In fact, we must crave to survive. We crave food when we're hungry. That's good. We crave sleep when we're tired. That's good, too. But when our necessary cravings are eclipsed by cravings for experiences that simply give us pleasure, that's not good.

This is powerful stuff that not only affects our thinking, but actually *physically changes our brains*. In fact, Lewis writes that with addiction, the brain changes "at every level: gene expression, cell density, the concentration and location of synapses and their fibers, even the size and shape of the cortex itself,"[5] so that addiction is like a spot in your brain where you've created a deep rut into which your consciousness keeps slipping and getting stuck.

"Addiction is indeed a brain problem," Maia Szalavitz writes in the *New York Times*, "but it's not a degenerative pathology like Alzheimer's disease or cancer, nor is it evidence of a criminal mind. Instead it's a learning disorder, a difference in the wiring of the brain that affects the way we process information about motivation, reward and punishment."[6]

You can be born with that wiring, I would imagine, or with a tendency toward it, but most of us wire it ourselves.

DRUGS AND OTHER DESIRES

Lewis notes that behavioral addictions "assume the same characteristics, the same trajectory, and often the same outcomes as substance addictions. Gambling, sex addiction, porn preoccupations, eating disorders, and even excessive Internet use have entered the spotlight next to drugs and booze..."[7]

So it is also true for super fans, political junkies, partisans, helicopter parents and an endless list of other obsessive behaviors. They employ the same neural mechanisms, entrench themselves in the mind, and sometimes even physically alter our brains, to make certain that the super fan will scream obscenities at the television, the political partisan will never compromise and the helicopter parents will smother their children to death.

From new toys to old wine, there is a never-ending list of things that we desire, that we crave, and that we therefore could also become a bit too attached to.

It seems we are all predisposed to certain addictions and not to others – and we don't know what those are until they manifest. So, if we were to go into every experience with this awareness of our ignorance, and cognizance that we are entering uncharted territory, we could be certain to avoid slip-sliding down into obsession, addiction and the like. The seed of that craving already exists in our brain; it is our job to recognize that seed will grow to the extent that we water it. Think about it. Be aware of what everything is doing to your brain.

All craving acts on, and alters, the brain in a similar manner, and no craving can survive your control, or survive never satisfying it in the first place.

I'm not an alcoholic. I drank way too much, but I don't believe I have a disease. I'm with Dr. Lewis on that. Alcohol beat the crap out of me. But that's me. That's my brain. Those were my cravings, my experiences and my choices. I'm certain those 65,000 beers changed my brain. How could they not?

Will I drink again? I would like to. When? Not now. Not for a long time. I know I'm not ready. I'm certain that after my first drink, my next thought would be: "I can get drunk again tomorrow!" That's kind of sick. I'm not entirely sure of how, but through introspection, awareness and meditation I believe I can slowly work toward an adult relationship with alcohol. Currently, I'm on or about the 8th grade.

And what of you? Your experience will be different. You can probably use alcohol without craving it much or experiencing many, if any, negative effects. Most people can. Your Achilles heel might be cocaine, sex, wealth, power, nasal spray (true), buying things, cheese (also true) or something else entirely.

We're all different and the desire to feel different is universal and can be a huge positive when we crave the right things and with a healthy intensity.

FEELING MORE, NOT LESS

As kids, we were told not to smoke marijuana because it was a "drug", which is bad enough, but it could be laced with something that would lead us to jump off buildings. I believe that was horse tranquilizer. Seriously.

So, while our parents mixed Manhattans (also a "drug") and warned us to stay the hell away from marijuana, we were watching kids wrap cars around telephone poles drunk off their asses, while the stoners were just high and listening to Emerson Lake and Palmer albums in black-lit bedrooms. It was rather obvious, even to our young minds, that marijuana was the least of society's problems, especially considering the perfect legality and social acceptability of buying a 1.75-liter plastic bottle of cheap vodka right down the street, which might lead you to throw up, fall down or die. It was like watching our parents fire machine guns hither and yon while shouting at us about the dangers of loaded BB guns.

I come to the defense of cannabis because the fact that it's illegal is ludicrous. When was the last time you heard about a marijuana-fueled tragedy? I know a guy who wrapped a beautiful, even exquisite Christmas gift only to notice, while admiring his work, the actual gift still sitting on the table. It was a tragedy, yes, but it's a matter of degree.

It's not that marijuana is harmless. In fact, while it has a lenitive effect on my anxiety and depression, it can also increase those same things in some people. Like any other drug, it's not to be trifled with, but unlike many other drugs, including alcohol, it cannot kill you.

It seems like we're already on the right path to ending the criminalization of marijuana. Legalize it, regulate it and keep it and all other substances out of the bodies and minds of kids under 18, when their brains are growing and developing in leaps and bounds. Protect those young minds for they are by far the world's single most important natural resource. Take that, fracking oil.

"Marijuana — medicinal cannabis — a painkilling, anti-inflammatory, metabolism-regulating, cancer-killing, heart-opening medicine. Side effects include a shift in perception, a dehabituation that may help you reconnect to the Earth, to your own body and to each other. Cannabis can help you to feel more, not less."[18]
- Julie Holland, [The World's Smartest] psychiatrist, quoted in Seattle Times

GENERALIZED

Anxiety is normal. We all have it. But when I was 18 and at the University, I began to experience heightened anxiety at abnormal times and for abnormal reasons, like having to cross another sidewalk at a corner, or whether or not to light a candle. These simple questions filled me with dread. I knew it was ridiculous, but there it was, so I tamped it down with beer, I think, and went on with my life.

My depression was typical – hopelessness, sadness, anger and fatigue. It wasn't all that severe either, but for flare-ups in the autumn when the daylight took a dive. Beer helped there also.

But when I wasn't drinking, say, at 3 AM or 3 PM, the anxiety would fire up again and I'd be gob-smacked by the sudden certainty that all of this – my family, my business, my mind – was crashing down around me. More and more over time it would erupt into my consciousness and I would physically start, shudder, sometimes even shout and, mind you, there are only so many excuses you can make when your kid looks at you askance and asks, "Why did you do that?" And you don't want to say, "Because we're fucking screwed!"

All of this, and some serious autumn blues (it was October in these northern climes), got me into my doctor to ask for some Xanax. Xanax is an anti-anxiety medication that I'd had in the past and it worked remarkably well. Xanax in; anxiety out. So, I figured I would get a bottle from the doctor and be good to go.

She said, "No."

She said she wanted to try me on a daily antidepressant to manage the depression and anxiety, rather than just treat the symptoms short term, which is what Xanax does. I told her that when I had another doctor, she said the same thing, and I did and I hated it. I told her it made me dull, unfocused, not happy, not sad, just blah, and so I stopped taking it.

She told me that she knew that, that she could see it right there on my chart, and that she also didn't like that particular drug, as it had those effects on a lot of people. She wanted me to try a different drug. I said, I don't want to try a different drug. I want Xanax. I liked it and it worked. She held firm and assured me that I would be taking the smallest dose of the Zoloft that she prescribes, and that she'd also give me a few Xanax for when it gets particularly bad.

I gave in, picked up the two prescriptions, and tossed the Xanax in my bag to be with me and the daily anti-depressant on the kitchen counter to be ignored.

The Xanax was gone in a week, and one morning I was feeling particularly awful, distressed, fraught with anxiety and quick to anger. I had just finished screaming at the kids for one thing or another. I was standing in my kitchen and noticed the bottle of anti-depressant pills on the counter. I picked it up and saw that it was Zoloft. Somehow that surprised me as I had already forgotten what it was from our conversation. I took one. And kept taking one every day.

In a few days, I had never felt better in my life, or better yet, I felt how I had forgotten I could feel – normal – which was a vast improvement from how I had been feeling. I just didn't know that what I had been feeling wasn't normal, and a drug that makes one feel normal was an abnormal concept to me until I felt it. I suppose that my depression had grown slowly enough over time that I never realized how much it had changed my mind until I took the pill.

I had been dead-set on not taking a daily antidepressant. In fact, I fought that notion tooth-and-nail for a very long time. But I did and it worked. Honestly, I had thought there was something wrong with the very idea. I was wrong. That antidepressant was absolutely right.

THE WONDERS OF DRUGS

Speaking to modern humans – and particularly young people
– about the wonders of psychotropic medications like Xanax
or Zoloft is like lecturing The Inuit on the wonders of fire. We
consume them in staggering amounts.

What struck me though is that I had a terrible experience with
the first drug and was helped immensely by the second drug,
which is quite the opposite from some of the comments I saw
online when I researched it.

I realize that's because each one of us is so different –
physically, mentally and emotionally – and our brains, in
their infinite complexity, are the seat of the drug reaction. So
every drug naturally affects every person differently and our
reactions to them vary widely. One person can use cocaine
for years and walk away with nary a thought, while another
might be destroyed by it in a year. I got immense help from
the daily Zoloft, whereas others complained of all sorts of bad
experiences and side effects.

[I'd be remiss if I didn't note that one of the possible side effects listed for both Zoloft and Xanax is hallucinations. I can't imagine either of those produced The Experience, but I think they'd be a lot more popular if they could.]

A month after I started taking the Zoloft, I suddenly quit drinking and it was far easier than it ever had been. I just stopped. If I quit drinking because of the Zoloft, did I drink so much because I was depressed? I don't know that answer, but it makes some sense.

The bottom line is that the war on drugs is an abject failure (making us 0 for 2 if you factor in the prohibition of alcohol in the 1930s). Rather than a war, we need to invest in learning more about how drugs work in our minds to build better treatment options and, as individuals, learn how to navigate them intelligently and carefully. Fortunately, or unfortunately, drugs are not going away. In fact, they're proliferating. Thanks to advanced technology, people are now making drugs with 3D printers, so that's handy.

And people are always looking to get (feel, think) different, to escape from the now and the normal. Viva la difference! Anything but reality – and there are many, many ways to get different.

Drugs are not a problem we can stop at its source without martial law, but we can stop them at the other source – the mind that craves them. That's the only true source and the only place it can ever stop, be controlled or, better yet, never start.

Meditation can help. In fact, meditation pulls you in the other direction – back from distraction and to the now or life in real-time. In meditation, we pay close attention to our minds and our bodies, and this helps us avoid bad habits, unhealthy obsessions and straight-up addictions. And do you know what we crave more than anything else here in 21st century? The one thing we seek out constantly, desire and satisfy over and over and over every single day?

That's entertainment!

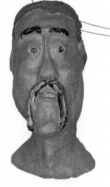

We are not addicted to our smart phones, tablets and laptops as is often maintained (that's like being hooked on the syringes). We are addicted to the sweet, mind-altering entertainment they release into our systems.

THE EXPERIENCE — I SEE GOD!

[The Experience, Continued]

...I SEE GOD!

Not standing in my bathroom, mind you, but the bathroom itself is God and so is everything else – God. Everything is God.

Moments pass and I'm frozen in the doorway, in wide-eyed wonder. Everything in the room pulsates with life: the faucet, the shower curtain, the vanity, the photos on the wall and, yes, the toilet. Everything is alive. I am certain of it. And Everything is God. It's all one thing!

I'm transcendent, one with the Universe, blown completely away; it is clear as the light that beams above the mirror; a warm bath of truth and beauty; sweetness and light. In fact, it's as if everything is made of light. And it's all alive. Everything is alive!

I step over the threshold and push the door shut behind me.

It is the most beautiful thing I have ever seen or could imagine, my bathroom. The colors are spectacular, gleaming and glowing as if lit from within. They bounce in the light off the porcelain and tile. I can see everything – every atom, photon, particle, material, surface, angle, texture and edge reverberates with life. The energy of life – God's life. It is all clearly alive. Nothing's inanimate – everything is changing and evolving! And so extraordinarily beautiful!

It is all that is good in the world, all love and compassion, kindness and laughter, happiness and peace filling my soul. No drug could bring me here.

[Let it be said that I was not on any drugs at the time.]

I look in the mirror and see myself – my corporeal self. My eyes are like windows. I look through them. I see that I'm like clay. My body is not me. I am moving, but not any differently from the shampoo bottle or bar of soap. This thing is not me. I am in here inside it.

I don't know how long I spend soaking up all that Godliness, but again I slowly become aware of bad things moving around in the peripheries of my awareness. During meditation, you learn to "see" thoughts arise in your mind, but this is something different. These things are black and curling around each other, like snakes in a bucket. They seem to be trying to stay out of my direct line of sight or awareness – rolling under and away when I glance at them. The glow fades.

I brush my teeth and walk quickly back across the hall to the bedroom, surrounded by black ghouls. I lie down on my bed and grab the nearest book – *"A History of God" "Irony!" I say, maybe hoping to wake my wife. "I think I'm going a little crazy here, babe," I say again, and again she sleeps on.*

I reach up and turn out the lamp, the room goes dark, and all hell breaks loose.

[To be continued…]

"Wonder is the door that permits us to experience irreducible complexity.¹⁹"

- Paul R. Fleischman

THAT'S ENTERTAINMENT!

I taught one quarter of writing at a university after I finished my Master's Degree in English, but that was it. There were too many PhDs knocking around looking for work, so I eventually applied for a job as a copywriter at an ad agency. I didn't completely buy in to advertising. I figured it only kind-of worked, and that people don't really look at an ad, stand up and do anything. But I also figured I could write that sort of copy and it sounded like fun.

One of my early assignments was for a local long distance company. At the time, you couldn't turn your head without being assaulted by an ad, commercial, direct mail or phone call from one long-distance carrier or another. Most of these were huge multi-national corporations and our client was much smaller, so the ad featured the head of a hippopotamus poking out of a pond with a bird sitting on his nose safely out of the water and with the headline that was something like: "Sometimes it pays to be small. Only 9.9 cents a minute." Cute, right?

The morning it ran as a half-page ad in the local newspaper, the account executive called me into her office and said she heard from the client that the phones were ringing off the hook.

I was dumbfounded. How could that be? This stuff doesn't work!

It wasn't even a particularly good deal so any savings would be minimal, but apparently if you put a bird on a hippopotamus's head, and say something mildly clever about the situation, some number of people will take action, make the call, and change their long distance carrier.

That would never happen to me.

You're thinking the same thing, right? It might work, but not on me. We're both wrong. Everything works on us – if it gets to us – mostly to a tiny degree (one simple experience in a complex lifetime), but also often very profoundly. Just by glancing at an ad, or watching a show in a bar, or passively listening to a radio broadcast, we give permission to make changes to our minds that possibly could lead us to do whatever it is they want us to do. That's advertising. That's basic communication and it works. And that's something we don't often think about.

It's not that we're suckers. We can't help it. It really is simple communication – my idea in your head. It's what makes the world go 'round and advertising work. And advertising works.

While we might think that we've come to whatever it is we've come to through intelligent and thoughtful means, that is probably not the case. We believe that when we pick a product, assess a person, choose a position, and the like, that we understand why we do it and all the influences that led to the decision. Surprisingly, mostly we don't. Mostly we're winging it, going with what we've been told by others, or succumbing to the whims of our own unconscious mind. And often we're wrong.

Certain words used in restaurant menu copy have consistently been shown to increase people's rating of a dish versus the exact same dish without the sweet description.

SUSPENDED DISBELIEF

We can all disagree on what makes a great film, but the mind-boggling advancements in the production quality — from the picture definition, the sound, the sets, and the costumes to the magic of CGI and computers in general — is undeniable. What technology has done for that which we see on screen is beyond anything that could have been imagined not long ago. Whatever one can think up can be rendered beautifully and astonishingly believable. This has opened a treasure palette of options that push us further and further away from the need to suspend disbelief.

When we suspend disbelief, as we do consuming anything from a book to a blockbuster movie, we ignore things that would reveal the artifice of what we are watching. Suspension of disbelief, which is just the ability to ignore the fact that it is just entertainment, is also why we watch. If we were unable to suspend disbelief, we'd be bored senseless.

Instead, we can experience real emotions in response to what we are seeing in the words on screen or on stage – joy, fear, excitement, sadness, anxiety, anger – which we would feel if it were actually happening. That's empathy. So watching the loving grandmother die on screen, while knowing she's an actress playing a fictional character on a set surrounded by lights, cameras and gaffers, can still lead to real wracking sobs at the sadness and injustice of her death.

But these advances also mean we don't get to suspend disbelief and, more importantly, we don't get to bring our own imagination to the experience. It's all there and entirely believable in every respect but for scent of grandma's lotion (which they are no doubt working on).

Enter virtual reality.

SOUND AND VISION

If we go to a theater production with spare sets, our minds work to fill in what we don't see. It's like that with radio, and reading even more so: we have to imagine the voices, the characters, and the settings. Our minds are active and engaged, and playing along, rather than just taking in a one-way broadcast of sound and vision.

I've blacked out (for all intents and purposes) watching television. I look up at the clock and hours have passed since I last thought about anything other than what the television was telling me. My mind is an empty vessel into which they pour whatever I allow them to pour. I once watched a video of a giant boil being purged on some guy's back. You can't forget that, or just about anything else for that matter.

What we hear and see – sound and vision – always makes an impression on our minds, becomes a part of who we are and alters us. It also scares, thrills, saddens, threatens, relaxes and tantalizes us. All emotions are fair game, and we love to be emotional. And each emotion soaks into our person.

Entertainment is a powerful drug. Just picture someone slumped on a couch staring at a movie on a big screen in a dark room. Now picture someone sitting there stoned. Welcome to the Entertainment Revolution.

Or try timing the length of the shots in a movie or television show. When they go to a new shot, count "one, two, three..." until they go to another new shot. You'll see how quickly they move from one to the next – and we can hardly wait for the next shot, but we always get it. Our cravings are satisfied over and over, the repetition fueling the craving fueling more repetition.

Life isn't like that. It unfolds much more slowly; it is not edited and the entire scene doesn't usually and suddenly switch on us. Although it can.

WE ARE WHAT WE EAT

These amazingly real, yet fictional portrayals can and often do make us wish and cheer for violence and even murder. It's what makes a great shoot-'em-up movie great. Mirror neurons – the same sort of neurons associated with empathy (in fact, it is empathetic) – fire and we are the shooter. We get to experience that fear of danger and impending violence then the incredible release when our gun blows a hole in the other guy knocking him back into a wall.

And if we repeat the experience over and over, our minds grow more and more accustomed to it. It won't necessarily inspire you to blow holes in bad guys, but your mind gets just a little better at – a little more in tune with – anything that is repeatedly impressed upon it, including each time a hole is blown.

Young people, bring that to mind anytime adults ask you to repeat something over and over.

The creators of all this entertainment have immense power, feeding the willing masses ideas, images, opinions, concepts, beliefs and whatever else they want us to consume – lies included. They can evoke anything in us, and, by wrapping ideas in emotions, push them deeper into our minds. You don't need to imagine what the words describe or read lips for that matter. You don't even need to chew. That's why they call it a feed. They can and do define, and also make mincemeat out of, what is commonly considered true, right or real. They can and do make the unforgettable.

Most likely all of this has something to do with some of the anger and violence we see in real life. We know that people are acting out some of what they've seen in the movies and television when they perpetrate actual violence. This is learned behavior as any other.

The great entertainment feed is no doubt affecting our minds. It's changing our brains as the shows, songs, movies; Lord, GIFs, posts, texts, and all the rest; become a part of us as memories. And they pile up in there – one after another – to create who we are and what we know. But I believe it's more profound than that and will continue to prove itself out.

There's enough entertainment – violent and otherwise – to keep us distracted for a million lifetimes. But again, it's not the content of that entertainment, it's what we do with it, and the choices we make. Violent video games and movies are highly entertaining and downright tasty, as long as we pay attention to how much of it we should each absorb as individuals. Do we want to be distracted for a million lifetimes? Or do we want to be very rarely distracted for the one life we got?

The power, beauty and spectacle of our entertainment, even on our tiny smart phones, affects us greatly – mentally, emotionally and even physically. It affects who we are to the core.

Sound + Vision = Immense Power.

The Buddhists understand suffering to be central to the human experience, and the eradication of suffering as that which will lead us to happiness. But suffering makes for good TV and so we seek it out – over and over and over.

PART GILLIGAN

Consider how profound an impression the on-screen fictional characters can have on a person who spends a weekend binge-watching a particularly compelling television drama. They will have spent more time paying close attention to those characters than they would most everyone else around them in a year.

I wiled away countless hours in front of the television as a kid. In fact, pretty much every second my parents would either let me watch or be unaware that I was watching. If one were to parse out my young life – sleeping, eating, school, etc., – watching sitcoms and variety shows would be an oversized slice of that pie chart. In fact, a very large percentage of the experience to which I afforded my developing mind was watching Gilligan's Island, Beverly Hillbillies, Mary Tyler Moore, Carol Burnett, Barney Miller, All in the Family, Hogan's Heroes and a host of other shows.

I certainly did spend more time with, and paid closer attention to, those characters than I did to most actual people in my life (adults certainly), and in doing so, I'm certain I modeled some of my own behavior after them. In fact, I'm positive I'm part Gilligan. I swear to God. I learned a lot from him. Nice guy, funny, incapable; and that's my M.O. Obviously, I would have been similar without the light of Gilligan, but Gilligan gave me the moves. You can't tell me I'm not a little bit Gilligan.

That's what I learned, what I exposed my brain to — repeatedly and in large doses. Had I studied physics instead of watching all that television, I might have my own teleportation device in the family room through which I could pop in on anyone anywhere at any time. As is, I can sing any one of the show's theme songs start to finish, which is sort of a win.

SAME WITH GRANDPA

Entertainment evokes emotions and emotions superpower ideas, embedding them deeper into our minds to become stronger memories. That is always the case. We remember the emotional moments much better than the mundane.

I'm certainly not on my way to claiming that everyone's going to be compelled to act out their violent video games, television shows or movies, but some are more susceptible to this sort of influence. We are unique, the mind is complex and it's only been in the last 40 years that our daily consumption of entertainment (much of it steeped in violence) has skyrocketed. Not to mention the fact that so much is consumed by children whose minds, attitudes and understanding of the world are just developing. In just a few generations we went from most people without televisions in their home to most people carrying one around with them, from no screen time per day to eight, 10, 12 hours a day and even more.[11]

And it's not just the young, according to Nielsen, retired seniors watch about 50 hours of television a week on average.[12] That's just sad. But you can use it next time grandpa gives you crap about your own screen time.

LIFE IMITATES ART – AND ART FOLLOWS US EVERYWHERE

Art has always imitated life, but life also imitates art – and more and more, I believe. We are immersed in it, schooled by it, led by it.

Who would I be now had television not existed? I couldn't possibly argue that I'd be a better or worse person. I'd be different in some ways, most definitely. More serious? Not sure. Less sitcom-y? Certainly. I don't believe all those untold hours had any real negative effect on me, other than making me determined to be funny and quick with the pratfall, and devouring an enormous chunk of my life that might have been spent doing something less passive. I'd probably be a better reader.

For young people, there's already a television or screen in your face wherever you go and there has been since you were born – the home, crib, mini-van, restaurants, gas pumps, waiting areas, the gym, and now Google Glass – serving up momentary lapses, delicious distractions, brief new points of view, and quick little highs – all the freaking time.

My generation could turn away from the larger world much more easily. Just walking out the front door meant no phone, no television, no screen, no texts, no emails, no anything that we needed to check, watch, monitor or obsess about.

Walking out the door meant letting go of the tether of home (and the world beyond what we could see and hear) and having at it. Now home comes with us — the whole world comes with us — wherever and whenever we go.

SPEAKING OF MY GENERATION

Growing up we had two telephones, both of them stuck to the wall. The only other form of communication was letters sent in the mail. We did not "overnight" anything.

We had one color television that was the size of a love seat. It turned on only after it warmed up. There were no remotes.

There were five television stations, all of which stopped broadcasting at midnight, leaving us with a waving American flag, an illustration of a Native American man in profile, or an atomic fallout shelter-looking symbol that on dreary nights conjured images of the end of the world.

Any other recorded sound-and-vision experience took place at the movie theater.

Our music came from our record players or full-on stereo systems – tuner, speakers and turntable – and was played with records (LP or 45); and then whatever happened to be on the radio.

All news came in the daily paper or news magazines, the radio, or on television at 5:30, 6 and 10 PM. Porn came in wrapped-up magazines with centerfolds and they were wicked-hard to get a hold of.

General information for research, schoolwork, papers, or if you just wanted to know something, was at the library, which required a trip there and a much longer trip through the Dewey Decimal System. If you were lucky enough to have a set of encyclopedias, you had the world at your fingertips.

We shopped at local stores almost exclusively, or occasionally through catalogs for companies where you had to call to talk to a woman who would take your order.

Back then there was no legal way for me to tell the world what I thought, and I thank God for that. Back then I don't think anyone would have cared what I thought anyway.

A POCKET FULL OF PUSHER MAN

Fast-forward just 40 years and technology – The Internet, personal computers, smart phones, social media, apps, email, search engines, e-commerce, and all the rest – has disrupted practically every facet of society and is not letting up. The smart phone makes televisions and records, radios and magazines, newspapers, home phones, and recording studios virtually obsolete.

And while all of this has given us immeasurable opportunities to be smarter, better educated, more informed and all that good stuff, 80 percent of what most people are doing online is watching movies and listening to music – pure entertainment, delicious distraction. Last year, the average American consumed 12 hours of media a day (thankfully, I guess, often doubling up; i.e., searching the Internet while streaming a movie). And even much of our communication now – texting, tweeting, posting, sharing, Snapchat, Music.ly, even Facebook – is also pure entertainment a majority of the time.

Even when I read the news online, I find myself in the comments section, gaining nothing of value, but enjoying the spectacle and sport of fake names hurling insults at one another. I also read the obituaries every Sunday and it turns out brain scans show that when we do, we are reading mostly for entertainment purposes. It is kind of entertaining. There are some very good obituaries! But I digress.

Fifteen years ago, those smart phones didn't even exist, but today they are as ubiquitous as they are revered, and hundreds of millions of human beings struggle to turn away from them, let alone turn them off. Your smart phone is like a drug dealer who fits in your pocket and always carries a plethora of options to keep you in whatever state of mind you desire. And it's perfectly legal and practically free.

This technology consciously works extra hard to lure us in – not only the content, but the software. Algorithms learn what we like and reward us with the stuff they "know" we want. This drug has a pusher man build right in.

But this technology and connectedness is so unbelievably awesome and we want it, need it and love it. In fact, staying out of the online world and away from all this delicious technology is not an option if you want to succeed in most careers – and will be even more so in the future. So we must strike a healthy balance, and remember that no one on his or her death bed ever said, "I wish I had watched more TV."

I'LL SHOW YOU

An old man lies still on a bed. A younger man sits on the bed next to him. The old man awakens.

Old Man: "What? Where am I?"

Young Man: "You, sir, are in the year 2026 and I am your great, great grandson!"

Old Man: "How the hell did that happen?"

Young Man: "With this!"

The younger man takes out a smartphone and holds it up in front of him.

Old Man: "What is that?"

Young Man: "A smartphone with a re-animator app."

Old Man: "A telephone? It looks like a lady's cigarette case."

Young Man: "It plays videos, searches the Internet, it's everything, Grandpa.

Old Man: That little thing is a telephone? Well, what do you know? What's an Internet?"

Young Man: "I'll show you."

The young man dazzles the older man as he takes him on a tour all around the smart phone, pointing out the incredible wealth of knowledge at his fingertips. He shows him family photos and videos, video games, apps, email and all the rest. He takes the first selfie ever of a man dead sixty years. The old man is beside himself.

Old Man: "A smart phone, indeed! It is beyond spectacular! The opportunities! The access! It's like a tiny door to everything! You must be the most intelligent, informed and advanced generation ever!"

The young man is staring down at his phone. He doesn't look up.

Young Man: "Wanna see a guy drive his motorcycle off his garage?"

Old Man: "Goodness, no!" He leans in. "Maybe."

"When we perceive the moon, the moon is us."[13]

- Thich Nhat Hanh, Buddhist monk, philosopher and author

CURATOR OF OUR MINDS

We are constantly curating our minds through the choices we make with media. Our senses eat information; our minds digest it and turn it into fuel that powers our thinking. Like our bodies, what we feed our minds becomes a part of them, nourishing them or not. So the question then becomes: To what do we afford our minds?

I saw a cartoon many years ago, in one of those wickedly-hard-to-get-ahold-of magazines, with a round-headed baby sitting on the floor and smiling. A scowling, angry man carrying a big black bag on his shoulders walks in, unties the bag, takes out a bunch of angry curse words, unties the baby's head, shoves the words in, and ties the baby's head back up, leaving him with the exact same scowling, angry expression of the scowling, angry old man. It's like that.

All of this broadcast media requires a counter-balance in our lives.

We should make sure we allow our minds plenty of time away from the feed and in control of our own sound and vision, to process and explore what we've experienced already.

THE EXPERIENCE — NOT FUNNY

[The Experience, Continued]

I'm not going crazy. I'm going to die! *The jittery thoughts explode from the peripheries to the center of my vision – all of my vision. This is no longer thinking, this is iMax. A barrage of heinous acts, bloody corpses, destruction, sadness, despair, fear and anger, flames and floods fills the screen. It's like some God-awful apocalyptic, doomsday, we're-all-going-to-die B movie. But it's not funny because I don't just see the suffering, I feel it.*

And I'm entirely powerless over it. I think of the end of A Clockwork Orange – when the main character's eyes are held open and he's screaming. That's me watching evil throw up all over the ceiling of my bedroom. The roar is physical. A hurricane beats against my eardrums. And it goes on and on and on, image after the image, atrocity after atrocity, after atrocity.

Suddenly, the bottom falls out. I'm certain my stomach drops two feet below me through the mattress stretching my windpipe. I'm gasping for air. Why doesn't my wife wake up? Can't she see this? I'm not breathing! *I remember the bathroom. I remember the whole God-is-everything business.* Help! *I try shouting to God or everything or whatever, but I can't make a sound.* Help me! I can't breathe!

It stops cold. I'm staring into black. Oh God! This is not cool! I've got no reference for this. Even LSD. Nothing like this has ever...

Wait! I don't even believe in this shit! *I glance over and see the glow from the streetlight below the window.* Okay, I'm alive. I'm here. Not crazy. Good. Dreaming. Maybe I'll just get up and...

I can't move. I'm frozen solid. I'm fucking paralyzed!

And it's back. The second feature engulfs me. Darkness punctuated by fire, bombs, explosions, screaming, burning, men, women and children suffering at the hands of every manifestation of evil imaginable. Again, it goes on and on and on, and I watch in pain, disgust and amazement. My fear makes me incredulous. What the hell is going on here?! *I demand of who or whatever is behind this freak show.* Stop this! *And eventually, for whatever reason, it stops.*

I'm in the dark again. This is way wrong. I'm the guy who always says that if God wanted to go poking around in people's lives, he'd have poked around in Hitler's and put a stop to the Holocaust – and certainly before messing with the likes of me.

"Okay, God, if this thing is real or you're real or you're really here or whatever the fuck is going on here," I think, *"show me your face!"*

Very slowly and almost imperceptibly my mouth and eyes begin to open, wider and wider until I'm certain my eyelids will split at the corners and my jaw will snap down to my chest. I'm frozen in an Edvard Munchian scream.

A great black silhouette of a bull's head materializes above me; a red mist surrounds it and spreads across the ceiling. It hangs there for a long time and I stare at it. (I mean, I would have even if I had a choice.) It is ominous, to say the least; somehow beautiful, compelling, but huge and foreboding. Heat radiates from it.

I wait, maybe for it to say something, but it is as silent as it is black. I don't remember there being any sound at all. I'm in real pain and grow angry again. What am I thinking? This is bullshit!

Boom! The bull's head explodes, shooting black shards across the ceiling in all directions, and in its place a succession of what had to be a million faces – human, insect, avian, mammal, some only recognizable as some sort of possible face. They seem to come from time immemorial and flash in front of me at an indescribable rate for what feels like hours and yet I'm certain I see every single one.

Eventually I can't take any more faces. Now I'm going to die. I'm certain my brain is about to blast out through my gaping mouth, and I scream: God damn it! I can't take anymore!!

The faces stop cold and I'm plunged back into darkness.

[To be continued...]

"Where there is perception, there is deception."[14]

— Thich Nhat Hanh

BE CONSCIOUS OF THE UNCONSCIOUS MIND

You see a strange face. You have a reaction. Not so much you, as your unconscious mind. It finds the most pertinent information that aligns with your (and its) goals, pulls it up, and the judgment is made. It is, of course, mostly a guess. But there it is. You didn't consciously think through who this person might be. Your unconscious just put them in a small, convenient box.

"The truth is that our unconscious minds are active, purposeful, and independent. Hidden they may be, but their effects are anything but, for they play a critical role in shaping the way our conscious minds experience and respond to the world," writes Stanislas Dehaene, in his book, "Consciousness and the Brain."[15]

We can think and say things we don't necessarily believe, we can do things we might not have consciously chosen to do, and we can believe things that are simply and obviously untrue.

That's just who we are and how our minds work, and when we ignore them, as we tend to do, the unconscious mind exerts even more influence over our consciousness.

MUSTACHES, PORN STARS, CONFABULATIONS AND RACISM

Have you ever noticed that if you get a haircut that someone doesn't necessarily like, they will generally demur, say something noncommittal or even float a half-assed compliment over to you? That's tact over honesty and generally a good thing. But when a guy grows a perfectly good mustache, people can be quite honest. A friend once told me that you couldn't trust anyone with a mustache because "they are hiding something behind it."

How is this? Our eyes perceive that little patch of coarse hair, send it back to the brain, and our unconscious mind tells us: evildoer, outsider, pushover, tough guy, gay guy, straight guy, genius, fool, whatever, so long as it agrees with our current goals and biases and comes from the knowledge we have acquired (and created) to date. Then we can jump from a clump of hair to "seventies porn star" – just like that. Trust me – it's not funny.

Our opinions are based on what we know and the less we know about something or someone, the more likely our biases will come into play. That's where racism, sexism, and all the other ism's come from. Logically no one could lump millions of extraordinarily unique people into a single – usually negative – opinion. It's entirely illogical. But if we just go with what we don't know and allow our unconscious mind to throw up an unfounded opinion that creates a negative reaction, we can definitely do it. The immediacy of the reaction belies the bias. It's a straight shot in the brain. Mustache = porn star.

As complex as we are as individual human beings, our ideas of other people, other than those who are very close to us, are blatant approximations, confabulations, cobbled together bits and pieces, around which we fill in the details – or not.

That's because it's exceptionally hard to understand people, but it's extremely easy to have an opinion about those same people. Do we know enough about someone to form a reasonably accurate and complete understanding of them on which we can base an opinion? Generally, not. Even those close to us are at many levels mostly a mystery. We know just a small percentage of who they really are, the untold thoughts they've had, or the experiences over their lifetime that we have missed. But like complex constellations drawn upon four stars, hundreds of millions of light years apart, we imagine the rest.

"Truth is a probability statement. When we define what we know we need to also clarify how we have come to know it. We always know what we know based on something, and that basis may contain hidden viewpoints and biases."[16]

- Paul R. Fleischman

BIAS MEANS NEVER HAVING TO SAY YOU'RE WRONG

Our lives are rich with experiences, but if we only spoke to those, or to things we know to be most assuredly true, we'd be mostly silent. So we just go with our beliefs. And those beliefs take shape as us, and turn into who we are, how we approach the world, and how we live, communicate and approach others. It's called availability bias: we work with what we've got.

Then there's confirmation bias: we interpret information so it agrees with our beliefs and convictions. And it gets better. We also actively forget opposing evidence more quickly, overstate our own knowledge, align our opinions with what we believe is the consensus, and on and on.[17] Need to add reference to bias book. Need to find book.

But with a little introspection, we know. Our unconscious already knows. This might be part of why we are so angry. We are perfectly aware that we are woefully in the dark about so many things we feel we should know, so we just fall back on our biases and others' (all-too-often angry) opinions gleaned from the Internet and television. The media is chock full of people screaming angrily at each other – from reality TV to 24-hour news. And as angry as it makes us, we still love it.

I got in an argument with a more conservative buddy about The Affordable Care Act. I told him that the current system was by far the most expensive in the world and yet one of the worst in providing care and needed to change. He said the act would lead to doctors quitting, care being doled out in some socialist nightmare, and even more expense.

Did either of us know with any certainty whatsoever that what we claimed would come to pass? No. Had either of us read The Affordable Care Act? No. Did either of us have even a slightly robust understanding of The Affordable Care Act, the current market, the medical system, the players, the specialties, the needs, laws, types of plans, costs. etc.? No. So what the hell were we doing? What we always do: parroting what we heard other people say, and what we then thought we knew, but what we really didn't know at all.

All too often, we don't have any real understanding of and cannot offer actual supporting evidence for our opinions, but we believe someone else has the evidence and understanding and that's good enough. And now there's the Internet. Every opinion – from the most well-supported and provable as true to crackpot theories put forth without a shred of real evidence or support – exists on the Internet. We can pick and choose, and so easily find someone who agrees with what we want to believe and, voila! We are right! Unicorns are real!

The Internet is a Pandora's Box flung open. It overwhelms. There is so much beyond our power to affirm or refute, except that which we choose to work to truly understand and in an unbiased manner. We have access to so much knowledge online, but we must seriously vet it, and be hyperaware of the biases of the sources, and those of ourselves. In other words, curate it.

It's amazing how often, when we ask ourselves the question, "Am I sure?" The real answer is, "No."

THE SAD THING ABOUT EMPATHY

In 2010, a University of Michigan team looked at 72 studies conducted over 30 years, and found a 40 percent decline in empathy among college students. Most of the decline took place after 2000.[18]

What?

We all have empathy. When we flinch seeing someone walk into a pole, or when we cry upon hearing a story that breaks our heart, or leap up in excitement watching a game, we are being empathetic. In our brains, those same mirror neurons activate and give us a sort of ghost feeling of what the person we are watching is experiencing. Empathy is crucial to loving families and friendships, caring societies, and just plain decent human beings. Empathy is why we take care of one another, and why entertainment entertains.

Thirty-five years ago, if a person walked into his school, work or own home, for that matter, and blasted innocent people with high-powered rifles, it would have brought the country to a standstill with mourning and disbelief. Fast-forward one generation and it probably happens once a week. We hear about it, cringe, and then we turn the channel. No one blinks.

I think we can admit we humans have a natural affinity for violence. Just ask any seven-year-old boy to draw a picture and it's sure to have a gun, knife or some blood in it. In college, on the first day of a short story writing class, the professor assigned us all to write a two-page story about anything we wanted and bring it to the next class. As we were packing up our things he said, "Oh, and no guns." The entire class groaned in unison.

We can't get enough of it! We rubberneck to glimpse a crushed body in a car accident even if, at another level, we really, really don't want to see it or want anyone to be hurt. We fill our stories with it, wear it like a badge of pride, and attach it to our heroes. And even when it just fills our screens, our bodies and minds react as if it were happening to us; same thrill, same neuronal charge mimicking the emotions we'd experience if it were us.

Is it possible that we are using up our empathy with all this entertainment? Is it desensitizing us to violence like some people claim? Is real violence less impactful when we spend untold hours watching fictional violence for fun? Is that where all our empathy has gone? We don't know.

But if in a generation we can fall behind 40 points in the

empathy game, isn't it possible to increase empathy 40 percent in a generation? 50 percent? Or increase the amount of compassion?

We can. In fact, meditation works for hundreds of millions of people around the world and leads them to be more caring, compassionate and, yes, empathetic. With meditation, in a generation, we could get that 40 percent back as well as create quieter, clearer and more focused minds. It will require practice – meditation practice – but the effects are well worth the effort. Make a nice, deep path for empathy in your mind.

"Some of us, interested in knowing ourselves more deeply – perhaps to make better life decisions, perhaps to live a richer life, perhaps out of curiosity – seek to get past our intuitive ideas of us. We can. We can use our conscious minds to study, to identify, and to pierce our cognitive illusions. By broadening our perspective to take into account how our minds operate, we can achieve a more enlightened view of who we are."[9]

– Leonard Mlodinow

ANGER, ANGER, EVERYWHERE

In "The Heart of the Buddha's Teaching," the Buddhist monk, philosopher and author, Thich Nhat Hanh, talks about the seeds of consciousness. He writes:

"In each of us, there are wholesome and unwholesome ... seeds ... in the depths of our consciousness. If you are a loyal person, it is because the seed of loyalty is in you. But don't think that the seed of betrayal is not also in you. If you live in an environment where your seed of loyalty is watered, you will be a loyal person. But if your seed of betrayal is watered, you may betray even those you love. You'll feel guilty about it, but if the seed of betrayal in you becomes strong, you may do it."[20]

We all have a complete set of seeds in our unconscious minds. Craving is a seed, as is violence, anger, and addiction, but also goodness, kindness, bravery and strength.

Anger is an important emotion. We need it sometimes, but not nearly as much as we employ it. How much of our everyday, run-of-the-mill anger could be calmed if we simply didn't water the seeds of that anger? How much is truly unnecessary and beneath whatever threshold an intelligent and balanced person (like you and I) should feel and display? How much is mimicking, bravado, lack of control, laziness, or just easier than thinking or being kind?

Recently I'm driving along on the freeway with my two kids in the old minivan and a young woman with long blond hair in a sweet little red Italian sports car suddenly cuts me off. She's swerving from lane to lane, undoubtedly texting "Piper." She flips on her blinker and jumps lanes, as if it will magically clear the lane, and I'm infinitely annoyed by the entitled, clueless punk.

She's right in front of my kids and me, and I shout something I probably shouldn't have. She jumps abruptly to the right lane and slows down. We pull up alongside and just having to get a glimpse of her as I drive by (why do we do that?), I look over. It's an older man. He has long white hair. And he looks terrified.

He slips behind us and exits into downtown past the big blue hospital sign. I then assume he must be going to the hospital to confront some awful tragedy. And why not? I'm on a roll.

ANGER ALWAYS HAS A VICTIM

Cars are a great metaphor for we humans. For as we are there inside our car, we are here inside our head, and, as we have basically no knowledge of what's going on with the person in the next car, we have basically no knowledge of what's going on in the minds of the people standing next to us. We can guess and be semi-right, but we can never know. So we act inside our cars like our minds inside our heads. We can be weird in our cars.

I water the seeds of my own anger all the time, but I'm more aware of that now, have some semblance of control, and it's much less common for me to scream obscenities at total strangers from behind the wheel these days. Anger is an important and useful emotion if we are aware of when we have enough reason (and knowledge about a situation) to warrant the effort of our anger, versus when it just feels good or righteous to be pissed off. Anger always has a victim. Do they deserve the punishment of our anger?

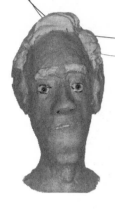

I have no doubt that our immersion in violent entertainment at least waters the seeds of anger and violence in us. It has made us better at being angry, and it has also inured us to some degree, maybe to an imperceptibly tiny amount, or maybe to such an extent that we cannot see the bloody forest for the individual atrocities.

YOU DON'T NEED TO KNOW ABOUT ANY GORILLA

There's a famous experiment where about 100 people were asked to watch a video of a team of people in white t-shirts and a team of people in black t-shirts moving around and passing basketballs back and forth in a small room. They were also asked to count the number of times the white-shirted players pass the basketball.

The video plays and the players circle around one another passing the balls back and forth. It requires some concentration to count accurately the number of passes and yet most of the viewers did. However, at the midpoint of the video a guy in a gorilla suit walks out center stage, beats his chest, and exits in the other direction.

More than half of the people watching the video never saw the guy in the gorilla suit.

Their unconscious minds did, and were perfectly capable

of making them consciously aware of the gorilla, but the unconscious mind knew that the job was to focus on the balls, and the gorilla wasn't important, and so simply left the gorilla out of the picture for the conscious mind.

They call it selective attention and our unconscious minds do it all the time. They see most everything within our field of vision, but also decide what should make it into our consciousness in light of our current goals – be they counting balls or getting drunk.

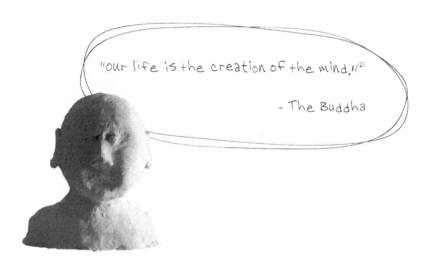

WELL-PLACED ELECTRODES

In "Consciousness and the Brain," Dehaene talks about a Swiss neurologist named Olaf Blanke, who stimulated a cortical region in the right temporoparietal junction in the brains of various people and created in their minds an out-of-body experience. Just like that. A little probing of some junction in the brain, and whoosh, they're up by the lights!

But that's just the beginning. Stimulate the anterior temporal lobe and you can bring back complex memories from the past. Stimulate regions of the temporal, parietal and prefrontal cortexes and you can create dreamlike hallucinations. Imagine the possibilities, and dangers, as we perfect that stimulation.[22]

We are what we think, and what we think can now – and maybe much more so in the future – be controlled by others on the outside. So I'm sitting here pondering whether or not The Experience was a spectacle put on by the creator of the entire Universe just for me, and meanwhile some doctor's poking some other guy's brain and he's thinking he's floating out in space.

The drugs of the future will be well-placed electrodes.

"I used to think that the human mind was the most amazing thing in the universe, until I realized who was telling me that."[23]

- Emo Phillips

LUCKY YOU!

Emo is right on both counts – the human mind is the most amazing thing in the universe and the human mind is who is telling us, and that is also why, not coincidentally, the human mind is the most amazing thing in the universe. We can tell ourselves things!

And you've got one too! You won the evolutionary lottery Grand Mega Sweepstakes Prize! Mountains don't get one! Chairs don't get one! But you did. And There! Is! Nothing! Better!

And, as a bonus, you can know it. You can revel in it. You can experience – through the wonders that are your senses – this life, world and universe with your mind. (You can experience your mind, too.) Your brain, mind and consciousness are the greatest blessings bestowed upon anyone or anything ever.

The feel of a child's cheek against yours, the smell of your grandmother's pie baking, a show of Northern Lights dancing in the sky, the sound of the wind through the trees – it's all in your mind.

Whether it's actually happening out there or not (and thankfully it mostly is), you experience all of it inside your mind, as we do our memories, imaginations, hallucinations and dreams.

It is the brain and the mind that create the soft-cheek sensation or the smell of sugar, apples and cinnamon. Your senses perceive but your brain processes and makes sense of those things so that you can enjoy them.

GRATITUDE FOR THE TOOL THAT IS YOU

It's an incredible tool that we each have. Each contains a human being, being whatever it is they want to be. That 3-pound ball of gray matter, the electrochemical exchanges, trillions of neurons firing, constantly, that is you.

Why then do we (at least plan to) exercise, eat right, condition our hair and moisturize our elbows, but pretty much ignore the part of the body that contains our actual conscious selves?

We've been given the Universe's greatest gift in a conscious mind. It is a gift that we can do with as we wish, but we should cultivate a sense of gratitude around that miracle and that little ball take advantage of its amazing talents.

The technology already exists to control devices using your mind: Paralyzed people are moving robotic prosthetics and college students are even piloting drones in competitions using only their minds and brain-controlled interfaces. Brain-controlled interfaces and all of their future manifestations, like all of these other technologies, will change the way we work, play and live. And, of course, they will change us. But controlling even the simplest device through those interfaces first means controlling your mind. Willpower is key; concentration, focus, and a strong, healthy mind.

Whatever you do with that mind of yours will be your contribution to the collective knowledge and the great history of this tiny planet, with these unlikely (as far as we know) beings that have evolved to write poetry.

THE EXPERIENCE — WHO SAID THAT?

[The Experience, Continued]

The faces are gone. I'm still paralyzed. I don't know if I'm breathing. It's dark and Oh, shit here it comes again!

Multiple, horrific scenes unfold at once on top of each other — a Technicolor collage of malevolence — and the images complement one another and amplify accordingly: A man burns inside a screaming woman's head, a house explodes when the switch is thrown for the electric chair — evil upon evil, suffering upon suffering. Repeatedly, I see lines of people, hunched over and shuffling in the dark, like shattered humans being led to gas chambers — stooped, broken, faceless beings.

This continues for a ridiculously long time before I finally remember the bathroom and the faces and the whole God thing yet again. Please, God, please! *I beg and plead.* I'm sorry for whatever I did. Please make it stop! *I go on and on and eventually it does.*

Okay, here's where it gets really New Age-y, but this is what I felt, and if I'm anything, I'm a stickler for accuracy (mostly):

I find myself floating in a bright, warm golden light, sparkling with shimmery flecks of pure silver, hugged in a snug silk cocoon, wrapped, warm and weightless. I forget everything – the evil, the images, the bathroom, the faces and my aching jaw. I'm between moments in time, nothing can touch me, and there's nothing around me but warmth and exquisite light. I'm free of all suffering, and of gravity. Nothing exists but this one moment in time and the entire Universe makes perfect sense. I am one with The Universe.

That's the only way I can describe it, and it doesn't do it justice. This is God's own ecstasy.

And as I bask in the sweet comfort, joy, and clarity, my mind wanders and I come upon the memory of earlier in the night when I had played the ukulele so well – far beyond my own abilities. I remember how good it felt when my fingers danced around the frets and my strumming was spot on, I mean, really spot on! Faster and faster. I was rocking that little…

And a firm voice resounded through my entire being:

"I did that."

[To be continued…]

"who the hell was that?!!!"

- Memoman

IN SICKNESS AND IN HEALTH

My dad died from dementia. He was diagnosed with what they call Dementia with Lewy Bodies. Think Alzheimer's and Parkinson's with often terrifying hallucinations thrown in for good measure. As I said, dad was a doctor – smart as a whip and cared deeply for and about learning, knowledge, science and the mind; and Lewy Body is a sick, sick disease of the mind. Fuck irony.

When Dad was first exhibiting symptoms, it was merely strange – sometimes even funny. He'd be certain he saw a bird fly through one wall and out another, or look across the yard to a neighbor's house and ask if we see the garden party with people in colorful hats milling about. We laughed because he did.

"Do you see those people down by the lake?" He asked one afternoon while we were having coffee at the kitchen table.

"No," I said and he looked again, then back at me.

"Do you see their dog?" He smiled, but I could see in his eyes that he really wanted me to see the dog.

But eventually it wasn't even remotely funny watching this man – who had more than a little insight into the mechanics of the body and mind – come to grips with what was happening to his own. He described hallucinations that grew more intense, vivid and complex. There were characters – three women and sometimes a man – who came to the house. They came to clean, and as he described it, "They were damn hard working," but they were also sinister and constantly berated him. Once they kidnapped him and drove him around the country and he escaped at a gas station. There were other stories with similar themes.

When he slept, he seemed to dream of the same sort of tortuous scenes. He lashed about in bed, fighting, protecting, running, who knows what else.

Sometimes his entire reality – the world that he was currently experiencing – would just "wash down" in front of him, revealing an entirely different reality behind it. He wasn't sure which one was real, and his descriptions were unreal and surreal, and yet perfectly real to him.

What happened in his mind happened to my dad. Those experiences were captured as memories and he recalled them with similar horror. They affected him mentally and emotionally to the same degree they would if they truly happened, because to him, they did. And there was nothing I could do for him.

To say he just had a disease that made him delusional or hallucinatory misses the point that those delusions and hallucinations were real, the effects of them on his psyche were real, and all those experiences were real, to him. And they became memories — vivid, real memories.

SWITCHING OFF

On May 24, 2014, I stopped in early to see my dad at the memory care center because my mom was coming to visit later in the morning. We had moved him there a few months before and she was preparing to move herself to be near him. The preceding months had been hell – for my dad, of course, but also my mom, who had also cared for him in the preceding few years as he worsened. His disease had progressed and the man I knew as my father receded to the point where I saw only glimpses and rarely.

I went in early that day and found dad sitting on the couch we brought from their house on Lake Superior, the one he always sat on when he was out on the porch. Now he was sleeping with a plate of mostly uneaten food on the table near him. The couch was all wrong in that room. My dad was all wrong in that room.

I sat down next to him and wrapped my arms around his

shoulders. He opened his eyes and looked at me, smiled, but then quickly disappeared again behind the same eyes.

"Dad," I said, "Mom's coming today."

He looked at me again. "So let's tidy this place up." He looked away. It was excruciating to see him scrunched up like he was. He had lost so much weight and seemed to be curling up tighter and tighter until he'd just poof out of existence. I loosened my grip and sat next to him.

"Dad," I said, "since mom's coming, it might be a perfect time for you to check out of this crappy-ass establishment."

I'm not sure if I was surprised I said this to him, as I had thought about it a lot. I love my dad, but believed in my heart that he'd be better off dead now. There was no quality to the life – just suffering.

"You've put up with enough of this shit, you hate this place," I choked back tears. "Shit, even the food sucks! So I'm just saying…" I paused and he was looking back at me, "we'll all be all right. You taught us how. We'll take care of Mom. Get the hell out of here."

I got up and arranged all of his things, washed his face, combed his hair and got ready to leave. I walked over and said, "I'll see you later, pops," and leaned down to hug him. He wrapped his arms around me, pulling me down and held me with more force than I ever remember. He squeezed and squeezed, then let go, his arms shaking.

"You all right?" I asked and he sat back and smiled past me.

I kissed him, said, "I love you," and went to leave. At the door, I turned and looked at him sitting in front of the window, the leaves on the trees waving in the breeze. He looked so very small. He was my dad.

My mom arrived a little while later. She had been terribly concerned that he would pass away when she was not there, and while she had planned to come the day after, she had this sudden urge to be there and came a day early.

It was a gorgeous spring afternoon. They had lunch and sat out on the sunny veranda among the blooming plants and flowers, and chatted (mostly her, of course). After a while, they went back inside and mom decided to do a little shopping before dinner. While she was gone, dad died.

When she returned, the nurses had already cleaned him up and laid him out on his bed. My mom called me, my wife and I drove over and we had a glass of wine sitting bedside, toasting the man we all love so dearly, thankful that he had peace. Mom was there. It was perfect.

I've told a lot of people that story and many have responded with very similar experiences. I can't help but wonder if we can, at the very end, decide when to switch off and move on.

"When people die, they cannot be replaced. They leave holes that cannot be filled, for it is the fate — the genetic and neural fate — of every human being to be a unique individual, to find his own path, to live his own life, to die his own death."[24]

- Oliver Sacks

THE AMAZING DISAPPEARING NICOTINE

One night at a dinner with family, I wanted decaf coffee because it was late and someone made some. After my second cup, they said, "Oh, shit, that had caffeine." I thought about it and could totally feel it. I was screwed. And of course, I couldn't sleep at all. Just lied there in bed, my mind racing, and finally dozed off at around 4 am. The next morning, I was told that, in fact, it was decaf coffee, before I had a chance to regale anyone with my suffering. It was as if I fooled myself into insomnia – I believed it so it became true.

Researchers at the University of Texas Center for BrainHealth and the Virginia Tech Carilion Research Institute got a group of 24 heavy, long-term smokers to not smoke from midnight to the next day before they went to an appointment.[25] Each person came on four different occasions where they were given cigarettes and/or placebo (non-nicotine) cigarettes. On the various days: the researchers told them the cigarette had nicotine and gave them nicotine; told them nicotine and gave them placebo; told them placebo and gave them placebo;

and told them placebo and gave them nicotine. Then they measured the effects on the brain and particularly the insula cortex – a key area associated with craving and addiction.

When given a nicotine cigarette and told it was a nicotine cigarette, the insula cortex fired the expected signals in the expected places. But when they got nicotine and were told it was placebo, the same brain signals were not produced. They (or their subconscious minds) were able to simply mute the nicotine high – at least in the brain.

The researchers' conclusion is that with nicotine, at least, believing has as powerful a physical influence on the mind, they said, as neuroactive drugs, and that we may be able to engineer belief states to better deal with addictions and behaviors.

The unconscious mind failed to fire "nicotine" because the conscious mind believed no nicotine was present, when in fact nicotine was present. Just think about that for a moment.

Placebos have been shown to do amazing things for people – or brains have, thanks to placebos. I see no reason why we cannot learn to control and utilize those sorts of powers, and then engineer our own belief states.

RELIGION IS GOOD

Did God summon my father to heaven? Or did my dad decide it was time and switch off? Consciously or unconsciously? Or was it all just interesting happenstance?

Did God say, "I did that"?

As I said, I'm agnostic in these God matters, but I've been to church. I'm a baptized and confirmed Lutheran. As a teenager, I took the bus to The Church of the Good Shepard on Wednesday nights and spent a couple of hours in the little chapel talking about important things. I enjoyed it. Went high once and really enjoyed it. But I quit the church the day after I was confirmed. Not in any big way, but just stopped going. I was fifteen and regular service was on Sunday mornings. We were incompatible.

But I do find it fascinating – and I did then, too. Church was calm, the music was lovely, the people were nice (if not a little stuffy). It's certainly true that religions can be beautiful and beneficial, inspiring and uplifting, seeking and loving. Some of our most significant art and architecture is a gift from the great (and small) religions. They offer billions of people solace and meaning; provide a refuge for those seeking safety from persecution. They are philosophical and spiritual laboratories, exploring, thinking, writing and sharing. They expand our understanding of the experience of life.

But I don't believe there is any reason a person should be expected to seek God, or even think about God, unless they want to. We've proven time and again that it's not a particularly effective or nice thing to force on anyone, and the idea that religion necessarily makes us better people was debunked thousands of years ago.

It certainly can make us better people, but hopefully we don't need it to.

BUT ON THE OTHER HAND

Religions can also become, not surprisingly, overgrown – complicated far beyond the original messages. They are often ancient and so replete with strangely out-of-date thinking. And they continue always to evolve, along with the generations of people, in unique circumstances, cultures and times, who adhere to them, add to them and alter them.

Many of the great religious texts have been written and rewritten in languages that were/are also evolving. Many include stories, myths, parables, and metaphors, the meanings of which are unique to each time and indeed each person. Each one of us brings a complex lifetime of experiences to them (often centuries later) and so understands them in our own unique manner and context.

You may share a religious belief with a friend, but the understanding that each of you has of that belief is informed by an entirely unique lifetime of experiences. Beyond that, you can even share an experience, but each see it from your own unique point of view.

Each of our lives (the sum total of all of our experiences) is uniquely ours and ours alone, utterly unknowable to anyone else. This is not some feel-good platitude (or existential loneliness), it is profoundly true. We are so complex and our lives, and inner lives, so rich that we cannot be anything other than unique.

Even the quietest life is a rich symphony of experiences.

SUBJECTIVITY

That is to say, we are inherently subjective. We only know what we know through our own experiences and the knowledge they bring to us. That is our own unique context. That is also availability bias. I say, "dog," and every single one of us has a completely different set of experiences that come to bear on "dog" in their minds.

Think about this: I walked to high school and most days a scruffy little dog would run, barking, to the end of his little leash that stopped right at the sidewalk as if he wanted to attack me. On the very last day of my senior year, I was walking home and the dog must have known that he had just one last shot at me. He took off running, hit the end of the leash, broke free and bit my ankle. Then he ran down the street while I checked my ankle and a lady stepped out of the house and shouted, "Did you untie my dog?"

If we can't have the exact same idea of "dog" in our minds,

how could we of "God"? Notice though that yours just got a little closer to mine when my story became part of your context. Think about that.

We flock together, but our personal understanding of God, if we have one, or want one, is always unique. Identical twin nuns raised in the same convent and sharing a room for 90 years, praying, meditating and studying together, will ultimately still have different notions of God – and dog.

In fact, every single person's mental construction of their religion and what they do with it is different. No two experiences are the same. Our beliefs change, as we change and grow and age. And the portions of our mind involved in our religion expand and contract over time, but are always dwarfed in a comic (and even cosmic) sense by the other portion – the rest of us. We are not only more than our religion, we are immeasurably more.

If there is a judgment day — saint Peter, the Pearly Gates and all that — I feel relatively certain that we will be judged by our individual actions and not by our group affiliations.

LIKE, SELF-PSYCHOTHERAPY

In fact, as individuals, we don't even have religion so much as a set of guiding principles and beliefs that are unique to each of us. These are the stories, myths, concepts, values and ideas we believe to be true, have faith in, or understand in a way that helps inform our worldview. Some may be central to our religious beliefs, others not so much, and while many of us share many of these, yours are yours alone.

Recent polls show that 24 percent of Americans identify as agnostics or atheists, or have no religious affiliation (34 percent of millennials), and it's not surprising in light of the stories that dominate the religious news these days.[25] A lot of evil is perpetrated in the name of religion.

But discussions with God, some higher power, dead relatives – these things I think are like self-administered psychotherapy. Not everyone needs a psychotherapist but everyone needs introspection, self-conversation and an ongoing exploration of their mind, intentions, and beliefs. These things can help. Meditation can also help.

POSITIVITY

The seeds of your spirituality can be watered or left alone. That is up to you. It is a practice, like meditation, and requires consistency to make a difference. I believe spirituality and/or religions are important though, in that unless we can find ways to expose ourselves and our children to discussions about big issues (morality, the golden rule, how to be a good boy or girl, why we are here), and not just as parents but as a community, many simply won't get it.

There is endless religious, spiritual and philosophical thought out there to explore and curate for your own mind. Look far enough and you will find ideas and concepts you never knew existed but that might change your life. You will find things you like and things you don't like; things you agree with and things you don't agree with; things you believe in and things you do not believe in. You will also find that they often have much in common. In fact, some version of The Golden Rule pops up very often.

The Great Law of the Iroquois states that every decision we

make should take into consideration its effects on the next seven generations. I think that's brilliant, and I learned it from a paper towel wrapper. (Which, it turns out, is smarter than a lot of our short-sighted politicians.)

Plus, at present, our knowledge-to-opinion ratio regarding other people's religion is way out of whack. It tends to be that we've read none of their books, attended none of their services, nor tried at all to understand what they believe. So we stereotype them by their worst adherents, or those who do evil in its name.

We should always have ownership of our spiritual self and our guiding principles. Listen to others, but ultimately come to our own conclusions. We will be conscious then of why we understand the world the way we do. And even if we are deeply religious, we will recognize that religion only brings a portion of our knowledge and experience to bear on the great questions of life.

RELIGION ROCKS

While religions are often about those great questions of life, we don't need religions to consider them. It was only when people congregated to talk, listen and watch that they became religions.

You can imagine in centuries past that places of worship were the only spaces common people could enjoy well-produced entertainment of any kind. The singers, speakers, choirs, dancers and chanters, not to mention candles, incense, costumes and sunlight through stained glass windows, all imbuing the sermon with incredibly powerful emotions, must have simply blown their minds.

And now here smack dab in the middle of the entertainment revolution, churches are amphitheaters with stadium seating, jumbo screens, rock bands, flash pots (maybe; it goes with the territory), lasers, light shows and on and on. There is certainly much more to our religions, but entertainment is still a very large part of what makes them compelling and viable.

My family sings a prayer before holiday meals. It's a beautiful poem, spoken or sung, and it brings a room full of mostly lapsed Christians to a place beyond where we all stand in a circle holding hands. It's joyful and, yes, entertaining. Amen.

Belief in these things isn't necessarily delusion (as many say) as much as a willingness to hope and to be open to using metaphor, art, song, story and faith as part of your spirituality, your belief system, and your knowledge to describe things you feel you know and inform your worldview. It is also a willingness to admit that what we know about life, the Universe and everything else, is next to nothing.

If God exists – perfect in all ways, all-knowing, all-seeing, always and eternal – then it really must be unknowable to we little beings on one tiny planet in one small solar system hidden within one of trillions of galaxies in an unfathomably large universe, possibly a multiverse, even while employing the spectacular, complex brains we've been given.

So don't assume I'm assuming any knowledge of this God. The idea that God is everything is not even mine, it's not new, and it's certainly unprovable.

Some believe, some don't and some admit they simply don't know. Gaze into the night sky. There are a lot of things we don't know, but aren't they spectacular?

RELIGION YOU CAN SWEAR BY

My sister lives in Munich, Germany. We spent our first Christmas there this past year – my family, my mother and the families of my sister and two brothers. On Christmas Eve we attended a service at St. Lukas Church. We were 24 in all and most of us do not speak German.

But it didn't matter. We all listened intently and knew it was good stuff, gazed upon the art and architecture, and sang as best we could. My sister-in-law cried. It had nothing to do with what the minister said or the lyrics to the songs, prayers and hymns. The entire experience moved us. It was beautiful, gratifying and inspiring. I imagined what it must have looked like 200 years before on Christmas Eve at the same evening service. The candlelight alone, flickering up to the gold sculptures and dark stained glass windows, had to be stunning. How could that not have inspired our ancestors to believe?

At one point, the minister said something that sounded like

"shit storm" and we smiled at one another. After the service, I mentioned it to my sister, who told me that the minister did say shit storm, using the American slang to make a point. Religion evolves.

"Hope, like faith, is nothing if it is not courageous; it is nothing if it is not ridiculous."[26]

— Thornton Wilder

EVERYTHING

In the bathroom, I knew it without a doubt: God is Everything. The idea overwhelmed me. It was right in front of me. And I still see it. Everything is made up of the same energy − is the same energy − and God is the energy. It's the same energy that was there at the beginning, the same energy that animates all life − you and I, the Earth, sun and stars. Take away the energy from everything and poof − nothing.

So, if God is everything, everything is God − the teakettle, the chair, the tree, the wind, the clouds, the planets, the sun, the Universe. Everything is numinous, mystical and spiritual, and it is all one thing.

God then is the mass and the movement, the shape and the color, the light and the shadow. God is the notes and the chords and the songs and the symphonies, and God is the silence. God is Everything. You. Me. That person over there.

Your knowledge of God is everything you know because everything you know is what you know about God. Names and numbers and memories. Everything you've done and do, what you've seen, heard, tasted, smelled and felt. That's all knowledge of God. It's all God.

IF GOD IS EVERYTHING

If God is Everything:

- I can see God's expression everywhere.

- God is revealed through all learning.

- I should probably be nice to everyone.

- I can have great reverence for all of existence.

- My brain is some intense God.

- My dog is even cooler than I thought.

- What we do to the Earth, we do to God.

- What we do to each other, we do to God.

- Everything is a blessing.

If God is Everything, we can see people as holy, mountains as holy, not to mention skyscrapers, black holes and butterflies, our best friends and sworn enemies. We can know that when we look into one another's eyes, we're looking at one of the most evolved and precious (no, the most evolved and precious) expressions of God that exists in the known universe. Humankind is a miracle of life and consciousness, industry and artistry, compassion and passion. God-like.

If God is Everything, God doesn't create, God expresses, and everything that you see and experience are expressions of God, not separate from, but part of, God.

God then is a master artist. It's just that the art is so complex we call it...

SCIENCE!

So if God didn't make the universe, but God is the universe and everything else, and if we want to know more about God, we need to know more about the universe and everything else, and that, of course, leads us to: Science!

The more we understand how the physical world works, the more we understand how God works in the physical world, and, in a particularly nice coincidence, the more we learn to be in awe of the everyday miracles – the unfathomable beauty, vastness and complexity – that is life.

In fact, if God is everything, and religions are the quest to understand God, then science is the religion of God-is-Everything, because everything that science uncovers enhances our understanding of the system of God as everything. Dig it?

Science is where the quantifiable mysteries and miracles are. It is where we can gaze in awe at creation, seek to understand how it works and why, and increase our knowledge of everything, while moving our species, societies and planet forward and not backward.

It makes perfect sense that many of our early religions were inspired by and imbued with scientific phenomena – the sun, the planets, and stars, weather, animals and even humans. One could argue that the sun is the only real god we know up close – creator and life sustainer that it is. Its gravity (energy) pulled us together and keeps us in orbit, and its energy powers life on Earth.

Scientific inquiry into the natural world becomes holy if we see everything as the manifestation of God. The very act of slowing down and putting focus and effort on expanding our collective knowledge of creation becomes a religious and scientific quest. We are surrounded by truths and miracles to be uncovered and astounded by.

Science uncovers the secrets of creation, of the Earth, planets, mind and body. It is through science that the deepest understanding of the system that God, the Universe and everything has in place will be attained. Science is a thoughtful, methodical study of God.

But while all of this brings up vast opportunities to better understand God, it still leaves us trillions of light years away from understanding God in any semblance of totality. Equal, in fact, to our collective knowledge of the entire Universe and whatever lies beyond (or within) that.

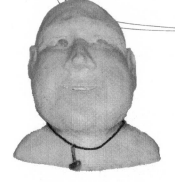

God is as aloof in this take on God as in any other take on God, but we have more God to work with.

A NEW SCIENTIFIC PEACEFUL GLOBAL ENLIGHTENMENT

Think I'm kidding?

Even if you don't buy any of that, science doesn't preclude religion or spirituality. They can complement one another. They both seek meaning, understanding, a strong base of knowledge and beliefs as well as proof. Science may not come into it when we discuss the existence of God, and religion has little to say about string theory, but they can exist side-by-side – both informing our lives and helping to shape how we think, act, and know.

When you think about it, science is the one true place where we can all come together as a species and work toward agreement while we learn, solve problems, and build upon one another's knowledge, failures and breakthroughs. It forces us to prove what we believe, and, if we're humble and smart enough to accept the truth, get along accordingly.

The Internet has surrounded us with so much bullshit that we can find information supporting ludicrous theories, and downright lies, so we need to be vigilant in vetting what we read. Society needs to be based on truths, and we need to be rational actors in the world. We need to embrace the scientific method, and support our ideas and beliefs with facts. Proof. And we need that coupled with the humanities, religion and spirituality to consider the things that aren't provable to fact through observation. Science and spirituality are the yin and yang of a complete soul.

Every scientist should write poetry and every poet should study science.

But scientific truths, real truths, the ones we can all agree on (You stuck to the ground? Good! We can agree on gravity then) are the ones on which future generations might want to base your societies. Scientific facts are global, whereas beliefs are not. Turn back to science, to truth, to proof, to knowledge, and when others fight that effort, you need to change their minds.

You will set the tone for generations to come, rid the world of ignorance, and usher in a New Scientific Peaceful Global Enlightenment, which would be seriously groovy.

Humanity recently reached the edge of our solar system with some time spent at Pluto. It's an amazing scientific feat considering we traveled mostly on earth and by horses 150 years ago. But beyond Pluto to the next thing? That's a rather long trip. For now, the Universe ends at Pluto in terms of travel destinations. We can see much more, but we can't touch anything else. We are all trapped here, but what a magnificent place to be trapped.

"Doubt is not a pleasant condition, but certainty is absurd."[27]

- Voltaire

THE EXPERIENCE — SAY WHAT?

[The Experience, Continued]

Say what? You did…what did you do? Who the hell was that? *My sea of golden goodness drains away and I'm left lying in my bed. But before I can stop to think: I think I just heard God!, the devil returns.*

Evil skitters around the sidelines of my mind, then explodes again, filling my field of vision. Crash, bang, boom, decay, murder, bloody corpses, screaming, crying, death, anger, greed, battlefields, burning buildings, crumbling cities, genocide, worldwide conflagration. It is so much information coming at me so fast I can't keep up, mentally, emotionally, I'm overwhelmed, drinking from a fire hose.

My eyes and mouth are still (or again?) stupidly and painfully split wide open. I have no idea if I even blink. And all of that evil sludge gushes through my gaping eyes, soaks my brain and drains right down to my soul. And again, it goes on and on and on before I grasp that I can scream for help, which I do and beg and plead, and eventually again it stops.

I'm on the verge of tears; angry, exhausted, and confused; shattered, trembling and absolutely fucking freaked out. What the hell is this? Why are you doing this? You've got the wrong guy!

My wife sleeps on beside me. How can she not hear this? *I can't imagine why she doesn't wake up. I turn back to my tormentor.*

What is this? Why are you torturing me? WHAT THE HELL AM I SUPPOSED TO DO?

And for the second and only other time, the voice speaks:

"Just keep doing what you're doing."

It breaks. I feel like I'm falling and suddenly I'm back in my bed in the dark. I'm dumbfounded and I become even more furious: What the hell does that mean? Do I really have a choice? I'm fucking paralyzed! And keep doing what? Lying here while you torture me? Playing the fucking ukulele?

The evil returns a couple more times, and each time I plead and eventually it stops, and finally it's completely over. I'm broken. I look at the clock and it is 3:38. I had come upstairs about 11:30. Four hours had passed, and I pass out.

[To be continued...]

DÉJÀ VU

Sometime in the mid 80s, I was spending a weekend at my parents' home on Lake Superior. It was around midnight and I was lying on the foldout couch in the front porch overlooking the lake. A big moon rose over the opposite shore reflecting on the black surface in a white river that ran straight toward me. It was one of those sublime moments of nature's stunning brilliance.

The moon bathed the room in light. I couldn't sleep so I stared out the window and waxed philosophical as the sleepless tend to do in the presence of a moon like that. I began thinking about the sun and how it's the sun's energy that lights the moon and sustains us. Then I started to think about how energy powers everything – from atoms to solar systems – and at some point, I hit on the idea that energy is God or God is energy. Again, it was not a new idea, but new to me.

There was energy all around me, and what it wrought – the

sun, the moon, the lake, me – inspired intense feelings in me. I eventually even wrote a song about it with a friend and these are (I swear to God) the lyrics:

"The energy came and the energy made,
matter became but the energy stayed,
and it practically hits you in the head,
it's time it should be said
your favorite god is dead."

Fast-forward a quarter century to The Experience and I walk into the bathroom and I am certain everything is alive, everything is God. I'm gob-smacked but, in essence, I had hit on the same idea (God is everything; everything is made of energy; ergo energy is God) just bathed in white moonshine rather than a luminous, numinous Technicolor bathroom, and rather less intense.

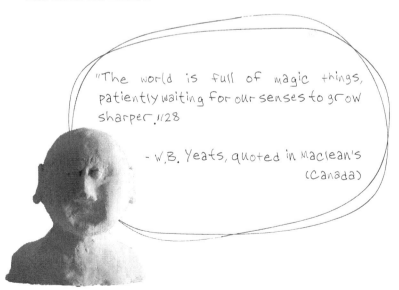

"The world is full of magic things, patiently waiting for our senses to grow sharper."/28

– W.B. Yeats, quoted in Maclean's (Canada)

IT MAKES YOU WONDER

I read an article about the giant sequoias in the Sierra Nevada.[29] The article talked about a particular tree – hundreds of feet tall with something like a ten-foot radius and on which exists an entire world of its own. Thousands of species of insects, birds, bats, other plants, moss and mammals make their home in and on the tree. And the tree itself – the article's descriptions and images of the two billion leaves, the branches and bark, the colors and scents, textures and shapes, and the moisture inside and rainwater flowing down the trunk – simply blew my mind.

I experienced wonder. I felt insignificant and awestruck at the same time. I saw clearly my place in the Universe and the incredible complexity and brilliance of the planet. I realized (or remembered) that life is an absolute miracle. The complexity of a single tree was more than anyone could possibly understand in a lifetime of study. One tree in a world of trees! I looked out the window at the trees outside.

There were many – each a world unto itself, each beyond my comprehension. I got goose bumps.

Researching for this work, I came across this in Paul R. Fleischman's wonderful book, "Wonder: When and Why the World Appears Radiant":

"One oak leaf is a tinker toy that contains more bits of properly aligned information than our minds can grasp. There is a universe of information necessary to activate the leaf. The forests of New England, or of anywhere else, are themselves like galaxies in which the numbers of properly covalently bonded atoms are far more numerous than stars."[30]

I had no idea. I can barely grasp what he wrote, let alone get my head around anything "more numerous than stars."

But that's the point. Wonder is always a surprise, a revelation. It is a willingness to embrace our own innocence, and our ignorance, and experience a sense of awe, connection, presence and surprise at the complexity of the universe. Wonder shines light on our arrogance while making great use of it. Wonder is active and engaging with the world; not just open-mouthed staring, but open-minded and open to, quite frankly, being blown away.

Our sun is the star at the center of our solar system, which resides in the galaxy known as The Milky Way. You can see the Milky Way in the sky if there's not too much light pollution. You ever look up at the Milky Way stretching across a dark sky and wonder how many stars it contains?

Roughly 200 billion and astronomers estimate that there are at least 2 trillion galaxies. That's 2,000,000,000,000 galaxies X 200,000,000,000 stars – give or take. Imagine that. That's a lot. This universe we live in is so very far beyond our comprehension. We are part of something that is so fucking huge we can't even fathom it, let alone: Why? What is it? Why is it here? What about you and I?

How can we claim great knowledge of God when we cannot even get our heads around the amount of stuff all around us?

IT'S A MIRACLE YOU MADE IT

And back here on this little blue planet tooling around a smallish sun amidst two trillion multiplied by two hundred billion stars, there is already more mind-blowingly fascinating "everythings" than any one of us could ever find time to marvel at.

To wit, your eyeball. The eyeball is an out-pouching of the brain, like a satellite brain, tethered a few inches away. The retina is like a bowl of neurons and it processes some of the information you see, then passes it on to the big brain to convert it into much more information about color (and why it's ugly), space (and why I'm claustrophobic), distance (and why I'm not walking way over there). That tiny squishy ball takes in and processes light, turning it into information and also joy: We can wonder at the Milky Way. We can't invent that.

Just think about the very fact that The Universe – all of

those bajillion stars (not to mention the planets) – began as an explosion, a great Big Bang of energy (as we currently believe and have much evidence to support), out of which the strong and weak nuclear force – and gravity – thankfully arose, creating order, chunks, matter, dark matter, galaxies, solar systems, supernovas, black holes, blue moons, red planets, you get the picture.

Fast-forward 14 billion years or so and some of the chunks eventually became the oak tree, the air that surrounds it, the soil that grows it, and the sun that heats it and nourishes it, not to mention, you. What began as pure energy is now your eyeball.

You and your eyeball are each a statistical miracle of miracles. It is enormously more likely when you look at the Universe that there would be nothing here at all. But here's this tiny planet that is orbiting a small sun, alive and teeming with billions of conscious beings – billions of statistical miracles. We should feel rapture at the fortune of our births when we consider the infinitesimally small probability of it all. Had two celestial chunks bumped together at a slightly different angle 8 billion years ago, none of us would be here.

But instead of empty space, there is this planet, and me, a being who happened to have evolved a brain and hands so I can work this computer, type on this keyboard, use this language and share my thoughts with you. I can move through space, run, jump, laugh, cry, love and wonder at anything and everything all around me.

This planet is a carnival of sensory delights: brilliant and beautiful, unfathomably complex and always compelling. And you and I have been blessed with a brain, a mind, and the senses to experience everything. That should be a holy shit realization for all of us – all the time. You don't need a ticket; you just need to open your eyes and ears, look and listen.

When we seek through our sciences – physics, biology, astronomy, cosmology, etcetera – and when we ponder the big questions of life, the Universe and everything else, we cultivate the attitude and open up to wonder. It is there that we explore the enormous complexity of life on our tiny planet, uncovering layer after layer, compounding more knowledge, and more wonder, about what's next.

If this is all just cosmic chance – happenstance – then it's the happiest of all happenstances. It is joy and amazement at the unlikelihood and great blessings of you and me and everything else.

It could have gone any number of ways.

"If you look deeply, you will see that the whole cosmos has come together in order to help the flower to manifest."[31]

– Thich Nhat Hanh

IMAGINE TRANSCENDENCE

Wonder is the emotion transcendence conjures and can be cultivated in our minds. We can become better at transcendence. Imagine that. Imagine transcendence – a lot. Some clusters of neurons fire in some order and we feel transcendence. That is not to belittle it, but to remind us that we are able to encourage it in our minds. Water the seeds of transcendence; open up to wonder. It is there that we see beyond to something much bigger than we are, something we may not entirely understand, or even understand at all. We don't have to understand a sunrise. We just have to stand before it and open ourselves up.

You know how when you're watching a movie with a genius cinematographer and a simple panning shot across a teapot on a stove is the absolute coolest thing you have ever seen? Life is like that, if you look at it like that. The sun shines the same everywhere. It's what happens to the light when it arrives that makes the colors bright or not.

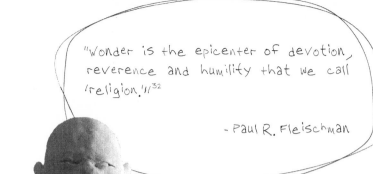

"Wonder is the epicenter of devotion, reverence and humility that we call religion."[32]

- Paul R. Fleischman

THE SALESMAN

Part of my doctor's orders, in addition to taking the Zoloft, was that I see a psychologist a couple of times to find out what else in my psyche might be inspiring all the anxiety and depression.

On the first visit, I told the doctor the whole story of how I had been struggling with the depression and anxiety, ended up taking the Zoloft, felt much better, quit drinking and started meditating and exercising, and life is good.

We talked back and forth for a long time and toward the end of the hour, he said, "I feel like there's something you need to do."

"Such as?"

"I don't know, but something."

I didn't really know what to do with that and we both let it drop.

On the second visit, he asked again how I'd been and I told him fantastic, and after a little more small talk he said, "I think I need to tell you something."

It was the story of a man who came to see him a few weeks before and not long after I had been there for the first time. He was in his 60s and said his daughters suggested he come – made him come – because of his own depression and anxiety, which they thought was due to the recent death of his wife, their mother.

The doctor described him as a very genuine, pleasant, regular, hardworking guy. And he was obviously way out of his element in a psychologist's office. The doctor asked the usual opening questions, and the guy proceeded to tell the usual answers: I was born here, my mom and dad were these people, and then he said, "...until August 6, 1973, when my life changed forever."

The doctor sat back and the man proceeded to tell him the story. He'd been raised in a tough house – angry, drunk and violent – and predictably he had gone down a similar path of alcohol and other drugs, fighting, petty crime and lots of guns.

That August night he was partying at a friend's house out in the country. It was late and at some point he started to feel anxious and jumpy and a dire need to exit the house. He pushed through the screen door and out onto the front porch, cupped his hand over his cigarette, got it lit, looked up and there was a man standing right in front of him on the lawn.

He jumped. "What the fuck are you doing here?"

"I'm here to tell you that it's time, Perry," the stranger said. [The doctor, of course, didn't share names so we'll go with Perry.]

Perry said the stranger looked like a door-to-door salesman – slacks, shirt and sport coat, no tie – incongruously in this front yard in the middle of very little.

"Time for what?"

"It's time, Perry."

"Who are you and what are you doing here? And how the hell do you know my name?"

"It's time."

"What the hell are you talking about?" Perry asked. He was drunk enough to see the humor in this but sensed an intense malevolence in the stranger. "Time for what?"

"Time to go back into the house and kill everyone, Perry."

"What?"

"It's time to go back in the house, Perry, and kill everyone in that room. I will help you."

"You've got to be fucking kidding me!"

"You'll be famous, Perry. It will be the biggest mass murder in Minnesota history. Now let's go!"

"Hell, no!"

"Perry!"

With that, the stranger lifted his arm and waved it in front of Perry who described experiencing every single pain, hurt, fear, suffering – every negative emotion he ever had – all at once. It nearly knocked him over.

"Now let's go, Perry," the stranger said.

Perry bolted past him and took off running across the yard and down the county road. He looked behind and saw the stranger following him.

"But he wasn't running," Perry said, "He was gliding."

Perry looked forward again and the stranger was standing five feet in front of him. He stopped short and the man lifted his arm and punched his fist into Perry's chest. Whatever he had felt when the man waved his arm was a tickle compared to this. Searing pain engulfed him. He screamed for help.

Suddenly, there was a bright flash of white light and the stranger was gone. Perry looked around and jumped when he saw the car idling right to the left of him. He hadn't heard it come up nor see its lights on the dark highway until now.

"You can get in, Perry," the man said.

"How did you get…?"

"I'm here to help you. You can trust me. Hop in."

Perry climbed into the car and the man drove off.

"Where are we going?"

"To the hospital. Your dad will meet us there."

When they pulled up, Perry got out and walked toward the doors. He met his father on the steps.

"How did you know to come?" he asked his father.

"Some guy called," his father said.

"Who?"

"He didn't say. He just told me to come here, and that you'd be here and hung up."

Perry turned back to the street and there was no trace of the car or the man who had brought him there.

I asked the doctor if he believed Perry and he said that Perry was a smart, soft-spoken, ordinary guy who experienced something extraordinary and didn't quite know what to do with it. In fact, he told the doctor that he had never told that story – ever – to anyone, and other than a few beers now and then, he had lived a quiet, normal life ever since.

The doctor went on to say that he hears stories like this occasionally, but recently, he felt, they were increasing in frequency.

"Why? Are we all going crazy?" I asked.

"That's the thing," the doctor said, "these stories mostly come from what I would call normal, rational people." Like Perry, he said, most are spooked by it and a little embarrassed and aren't even certain that it ever happened or even what actually happened.

We talked about all of it, delving into spirituality, religion, good and evil, devils and angels.

"I felt like I needed to tell you that," he said to me again. "I don't know why."

Three weeks later I had The Experience, and although it took me a couple of days to remember Perry's story, when I did I saw the similarities.

So I went into my next visit with the doctor and handed him the story of The Experience as I had written it down the morning after. Then I only half-jokingly accused him of some sort of psychological shenanigans, suggestive manipulation, the planting of ideas and all that. He assured me that was not the case, but that it is entirely doable, which doesn't surprise me anymore.

I sat nervously as he read the story. I assumed that he was thinking that I was making all this up, and that I just might turn into an interesting patient after all. But he was very thoughtful and read it all the way through, asked some questions, and then said, "I think you need to do something, but I don't know what it is."

"Yeah, you said that," I said. "Play the ukulele?"

He didn't laugh. "Something else."

I ran out of money and insurance wasn't covering it so that was the last time I saw the doctor.

I wonder. Did we evolve to have these sorts of spiritual experiences – full-blown hallucinations even – to shake us out of negative or hurtful states of being or when the unconscious feels we need to get our shit together?

We've evolved in all sorts of remarkable and complicated manners. If God has a plan, it's got to be evolution.

CRUISE CONTROL

When I learn a song on the ukulele, first I cannot play it. Then I learn the chords and practice playing those over and over, and get the transitions right; slowly, my fingers start to do what I'm expecting them to do and it smoothens out as I continue to practice, and finally I can play it all the way through with no mistakes. That's great, but eventually, if I keep practicing and repeating the song, I can play it without even consciously thinking about playing it. Then I can focus on the lyrics or what's for lunch.

That's the learning process. Anil Ananthaswamy describes the process in an article in *New Scientist* magazine. When you undertake an action, the prefrontal cortex communicates with the striatum, "which sends the necessary signals to enact the movement. Over time, input from the prefrontal circuits fades, to be replaced by loops linking the striatum to the sensorimotor cortex. The loops, together with the memory circuits, allow us to carry out the behavior without having to think about it."33

Tricky! This, you can imagine, is also complicit in our addictions.

The other evening I'm driving down the freeway and the traffic is heavy – four lanes of dozens of vehicles in both directions. In front of me, pairs of synchronized brake lights snake up a long hill, curving right, then left. The panorama is lit pink and orange from the sunset behind me. The cars, trucks, buses and semis are not 30 feet apart, moving at 10 feet per second in perfect unison and with flawless execution; and it struck me, watching this impeccably timed and exquisitely executed auto ballet, that many of these drivers were mostly unconscious of driving at all.

NATURALLY HAPPY

Life is loud. City life is ridiculous. There is noise from the moment we wake until we go to bed and even while we sleep. I mentioned that I lived a half-block from train tracks. The trains go by a few times an hour and 24 hours a day. The sound can stop conversations. Cars, trucks, buses, deliveries, construction, kids and adults make up the rest of the din. But then there's the furnace going on and off, fans blowing, the refrigerator's hum, lights buzzing, televisions, radios and all the inside noise of a small family.

Light pollution surrounds us as well. If the curtains aren't shut completely a streetlight shines right in to my eyes when I try to sleep, there are glowing clocks, nightlights in hallways, light from outside and bright little dots on technology that is supposedly turned off.

And then there are the graphics, more and more images, pictures, logos, words, video, screens, phones, lights, pixels –

all battling for our attention, pulling us this way and that, and making us (think, feel, be) different, whether we like it or not.

And yet most of us mostly seek it out. We cluster in large noisy cities filled with people, lights and machinery that never sleep, turn off or shut down – because that's where the action is, and more importantly, the jobs.

Yet we humans spent the other 99.9 percent of our millions of years of evolution in relative quiet – mostly silence, in fact, but for the noises of nature. There were no radios or speakers, televisions or computers, streetlights, cars, trains and buses, front loaders, backhoes, lawnmowers, jackhammers, factories, power plants, movie houses, and so much more that makes up the racket of modern life. Quiet is really a natural state for us and, I believe, crucial to a peaceful, clear-thinking society.

But quiet doesn't come about naturally, or easily, for most of us. We have become so accustomed to noise that we no longer hear it for what it is, and in fact, we desire it, seek it out, and even amplify it with our own noisemaking, creating distractions within distractions.

Plus, few of us live near a forest where we can find a spot on a little stream far away from the racket of the modern world. But we should try. According to the EPA, adults spend 93 percent of their lives in a building or in a vehicle. A lot of children spend less than a half-hour playing outside … *each week*.[34] This is not natural.

I read about a group of Korean researchers who watched

the brain activity of people looking at pictures. When the volunteers viewed urban scenes, researchers saw more blood flow to the area of the brain that processes fear and anxiety. Natural photos brought more blood to the areas associated with empathy and altruism.[35]

Spending time in natural environments allows us to really chill out, because it "doesn't require a prolonged effort or an act of will to avoid distractions. Researchers say this kind of focus allows the brain to disengage and restore its capacity for directed attention."[36]

So in a way you have to space out to get smart. Huh.

Spending time in natural environments can do wonders for stress, anxiety, depression, and even violent behavior. Dutch researchers even saw a lower incidence of 15 diseases, ranging from depression, anxiety and migraines to heart disease and asthma, among people who live within a half-mile of large parks, forests, lakes, and other natural settings.[37] It seems we do well by being immersed in other living things.

When we walk in the woods, we experience involuntary attention, where we don't have to make an effort to avoid distractions, which allows the brain to disengage from distractions and to be present in the world.

Meditation and mindfulness also allow us, and even train us, to be similarly disengaged from distractions and present in the here and now.

"All of man's misery comes from his incapacity to sit alone in an empty quiet room."[38]

- Blaise Pascal, quoted in TheWeek.com

THERE IS NO SUCH THING AS MEDITATION

That's because meditation is not one thing, but a lot of things, including a walk in the woods.

I first came upon meditation when I was about eight years old. I was playing with a friend in his basement when his mom called him upstairs. He came back down and said, "I have to go upstairs and meditate."

What? He might as well have said, "I'm going upstairs to levitate in my spaceship."

I didn't know meditate from metallurgy, but I knew it was freaky, and when I went home and told my mom she said, "Oh, yeah, his mom's into transcendental meditation."

Trancendental what?

It came up again with my cool hippy older cousins, one of

whom, along with his roommates, wallpapered their entire apartment with aluminum foil and hung their turntable with fishing line so it looked like it was floating but also wouldn't skip when someone walked across the wood floor or a bus went by outside. Brilliant. They meditated, so I knew I would one day too.

In my 20s, I had a relaxation tape with ambient music and a lovely woman's voice, who said softly, "Your forehead is smooth and cool." I liked that. It didn't call itself meditation, but it was about focus, relaxation, and achieved both. I got rid of my cassette deck so that ended.

Fast-forward 15 years and I've quit drinking, for a day, and it hit me that meditation might help so I asked my wife to teach me. She had done it a little in her early years. She sat me down with a candle and got me to focus on my breath and we sat quietly for a while and I liked it.

I went online and ordered a CD with some meditations led by a guy with Scottish accent that sounded cool, and took off meditating. Doing something with my mind, and specifically meditation, was my replacement for the effects of drinking with my mind. It was something different to do with my brain that was not: soak in beer. It worked for three months.

The four meditations on the CD were about breathing and lovingkindness, as well as a walking meditation and a body scan meditation.39 I practiced the breathing meditation for a couple of months and then moved on to the other three, and mixed them up. I was addicted. Soon I could recite the meditations along with the Scottish guy so I stopped with the CDs and just turned on some ambient music. Then I learned to lead my own meditations, and to lead my own mind.

At its most basic, meditation is sitting down and shutting up, which isn't easy. Think of when your parents suggested a game of "let's see who can stay quiet the longest" in the car. That didn't last long. We are communicators at heart – homo communicato (or something like that).

So when we really stop, close our eyes and be quiet (and not when we're tired), it doesn't feel natural. It feels like we're missing something. We're immediately bored. But it's much more natural than we realize. Our history, as noted, is millions of years of quiet, then a few hundred years of increasing raucousness, and something's missing for a lot of us. It is in our nature to need more quiet time because only there can we introspect, think (and not-think) and meditate. We owe it to our brains to power down the consciousness and allow it occasionally to rest and reboot.

Meditation is not about religion. It's about quieting your mind, listening to it, learning about it, and as a side effect, increasing your ability to lead it, rather than vice versa.

Meditation is a practice and not necessarily a religious practice. It certainly can be. You can bring your religion to your meditation practice or your practice to your religion. Meditation can be like prayer, even if you are not religious. You might express prayers of thanks to whom or whatever – it doesn't matter. Being thankful is good for the soul.

MEMOMAN'S 6 STEPS TO CERTAIN ENLIGHTENMENT (MAYBE)

As I said, I only know as much about meditation as my experience has granted me. It's not a lot. And meditation means so many things and can be done in so many ways.

But there is plenty of information to be had. You can find a teacher, join a group, pop in an MP3, become a Buddhist and move to Tibet, or just sit down and do it. As with anything, I would recommend seeking, learning and gaining a good understanding of what's out there and then tailoring it to yourself, and then seeking some more.

But your real learning will come through your practice, through repetition. It's your mind. You're in charge. If you are new to meditation and looking for a primer, read on:

1. Find a comfortable and quiet (as possible) place where you can be uninterrupted. Dark or light, inside or outside,

whatever your preference, or wherever you are. Sit on a cushion or pillow to elevate your butt a few inches off the ground. Cross your legs or employ the more complex and sometimes painful lotus or half-lotus. I've mastered the latter. It helps keep my back straight. The former is out of the question.

2. You can sit in a chair as well, or lie down, but you want to be comfortable and with a relatively straight back, \ keeping your chest open and your hands cupped in your lap or palms down on your knees. Balance your head on top of your spine, leaning neither forward nor backward.

3. Take a few deep, slow breaths, and relax. Breathe naturally.

4. Feel the weight of your body pushing down into the ground as you exhale, gravity's energy gently pulling on every ounce of you. Keep breathing. Close your eyes and relax further. Don't pressure yourself. Try not to think, but know that you will. Recognize but don't focus on your thoughts as they arise. Don't follow them or encourage them. Just watch them. And allow them to pass by like clouds through a clear blue sky.

5. Begin by focusing your attention instead on your breathing – the air repeatedly going in and out, over and over. Don't try to control it; simply pay attention to the air going in and out of your body. Count your breaths: "in/out – one, in/out – two…" up to 10 and then start over again. In the beginning, you probably won't make it past five before you've wandered into one thought or another, and/or

before you suddenly find yourself counting "in/out – 16", but simply go back to one and begin again. Don't pressure yourself. It's a practice and it takes time to tame the wild mind.

6. You can also focus on thoughts or emotions, sensations in your body, or even scan your entire body inside and out. The idea is to continue to bring your mind back to the here and now. To be aware of yourself right now. To be, as they say, *present*. I have a meditation that simply goes: In: "I am here." Out: "It is now."

> Even if all you do in the beginning is sit quietly for 10 minutes every day, you'll soon feel the benefits. I meditate about a half-hour each day (sometimes 10 minutes and sometimes an hour), which is not a lot of time to do something that feels good to do, and continues to benefit you long afterward.

ON THE PATH TO ENLIGHTENMENT, EVERY STEP'S A LITTLE BRIGHTER.[TM]

They say meditation can lead to enlightenment, but whether or not we achieve total enlightenment a la the Buddha, we will become more enlightened every day that we meditate, bringing us increasing joy and contentment, awareness, knowledge, and power.

You will achieve a stronger sense of equanimity, or psychological stability and calmness, when you face strong emotions, pain and whatever else is messing with your mind. Equanimity gives us personal peace, and it gives those around us peace, as well. Equanimity requires strength, but derives its power from peace.

The only place you will ever find happiness, peace, equanimity or anything else, is in your mind. Every moment you have on this planet, with which you engage with your mind, is more precious than a thousand hours of distraction.

I'm completely serious when I say that more meditation will lead to less violence, heartache, ignorance and suffering, and more wonder, peace, knowledge and compassion. It really is that good.

OTHER RANDOM AND PLEASING EFFECTS

Meditation lays clear the absurdity of our reasoning, constant thought interruptions, pointless negativity and anger, repetition of obsessions, and our conscious and unconscious weirdness. If you look closely, your mind will never cease to amaze you. We are all freaky in the head.

You become a witness to yourself. You will not love everything you see, but you will learn what to fix and to find joy in yourself, your life, everywhere and all around you.

You become better aware of your own filters, biases and misperceptions, and begin to recognize patterns, attitudes, ideas and lots of errors. And the recognition itself can be the solution. Recognizing that you are angry, looking straight at your anger, often drains it of power. You become less stressed because you see more clearly what really matters, and the small matters that give you such heartache melt away.

- You stop feeling bad about the past and fearful of the future.

- You will be more present more often.

- You can become the person you really want to be, even if you don't know what that is when you begin. Meditation can help you figure it out. It's that good.

- You become one with the Universe because you become one with your mind, and for all intents and purposes, your mind is your Universe.

- You learn to control your mind, but you don't wrestle control over it; instead your mind becomes easier to lead because you consciously work to understand your unconscious better. You bring your conscious and unconscious minds closer together.

In addition to much research that has shown that meditation increases well-being, makes people happier and improves quality of life, a recent study reported in *Psychiatry Research: Neuroimaging* has shown that people who meditated for about a half hour a day for only eight weeks had measurable changes in gray-matter density in the areas of the brain associated with memory, stress, sense of self and empathy.[41]

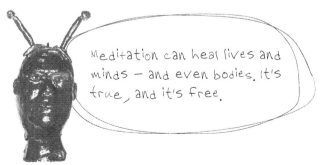

Meditation can heal lives and minds — and even bodies. It's true, and it's free.

THE EXPERIENCE — JANUARY 31, 2015

[The Experience, Continued]

What the hell was that?

That was my first thought when I awoke the morning after The Experience. My second thought was, Ouch. I was sore all over, stiff in the arms, chest, shoulders, neck, jaw, back and butt. I struggled to get out of bed, then went straight to the basement and wrote it all down. I wanted to capture what I remembered before it went away. Then it was out to breakfast with my wife and kids, where I whispered an edited version to her. She gave me a look.

"I was not high," I whispered.

"Dreaming?"

"Possibly, but I remember it all vividly and it doesn't feel like a dream," I

said. "It feels like pain. And it was way too long for a dream. And the whole thing started before I went to bed."

I looked around the restaurant and it was still there, albeit subdued from the night before – the glow, the motion, the fact that I could see plain as the pancakes on my plate (and including the pancakes on my plate) that everything was alive and in motion. Faces radiated. The silverware sparkled. Everything was one thing and it all still made sense somehow, except The Experience itself.

What happened? Was it just a dream? A hallucination of some kind? The first glimpse into the Lewy Body disease I'm certain I've inherited from my dad? Or was it God? Aphrodite? David Bowie? Or was it aliens?

I Googled it.

The first thing I learned is that it happens often, to all sorts of people, and even featuring similar elements — good and evil, paralysis, golden glow, feelings of being one with the Universe, among them. As unfathomably strange as it was for me that night – terrifying and exhilarating – The Experience is apparently common.

Huh.

WHAT ON EARTH?

Well, I'm a common man and I'm not lying. The Experience transpired on that night as I've described – be it in my home or merely in my mind. I can't prove it, obviously, but it rattled me to the bone. As I have said, everything changes us, and this changed me.

But I still don't know from whence it came! It felt a bit like LSD, but I was not on any drugs. Was it simply a very, very intense dream? As I said, it started before I went to bed. Was it the Zoloft? The Xanax? The combination? The death of my father?

Or was it actually God, creator of all things, white beard and all? Or another God? Did my sudden sobriety call forth Mars and Aphrodite to battle it out for my soul? Or maybe some lower god that isn't necessarily quite God but does god-like things around this neck of the Universe?

Was it actually my father who told me to just keep doing what I'm doing? Didn't much sound like him though. Did the psychologist plant the seed that blossomed into my brush with Heaven and Hell? He said he didn't, but maybe he planted that, too. What about my meditation? Did it affect my mind in such a manner as to make it possible for such a long and intense hallucination? Did it need to? Was Dr. Olaf under my bed, poking around in my brain and conducting a symphony of good and evil?

I have no idea and I'm totally cool with that. I'm glad it happened. I can still remember how I felt when I flipped the bathroom switch and Bam! Everything's alive! And everything is God! God is everything! I get it still – it's all moving, it's all alive, it's all God.

Not that I walk around singing "God Is Everything" all the time, but if I bring it to mind, or it is brought to mind, or the mind brings it up, I still get it. It still makes sense to me. And that's exactly where it all happened for me in the first place – in my mind, in my brain.

So even if my ceiling really was the site of all that gruesome mayhem, and even if I did float in a cozy golden cocoon while my wife slept on below, for me it all nevertheless happened in my mind, which is where everything happens for us. That is why the mind is so important and why we need to pay more attention to it.

I don't suppose I'll ever know the answers, unless there is a heaven and I get to put the questions to God, or sub God, an angel or St. Peter, but there's plenty of hard scientific evidence pointing to it possibly coming from my own mind. My mind was certainly capable of all of it. Hallucinations are real.

But there are also thousands of years of human study, belief, faith, and similar (and not at all similar) experiences like mine. Could all of these experiences be just some sort of temporary mental illness, or delusion, or a mass hallucination? Is there an evolutionary explanation to it? Maybe I had reached that critical point in my life where the brain had evolved to know to hit me with a full-blown religious experience and a swift kick toward individuation – like for Perry. *That'll set him straight!*

And it came out of nowhere. There was no plea on my part for God's assistance, grace or meddling. I was just sitting there (literally), minding my own mind, feeling perfectly fine, and I get dragged through heaven and hell and back, over and over again, and then God commands: "Just keep doing what you're doing." That's good advice when you're feeling perfectly fine, I suppose, but the timing then was rather off.

Maybe it was the meditation as to what "just keep doing what you're doing" meant, considering I was meditating when it all started. But again, it seems odd to interrupt my meditation, chase me upstairs, torture and tantalize me for a few hours, then say, "Just keep meditating."

Stay sober? Sober people have been known to have had religious experiences – although would that not come before (and in order to inspire) the quitting (like for Perry) rather than two months after quitting?

And what was the point of "I did that?" Why would this real or imagined God hijack my hands to make me play the ukulele better? To show me what I'm capable of? Or what God is capable of? But then this God went on to show it with much more gusto through the four hours of late-night hell raising. The ukulele jam didn't quite measure up to the golden cocoon.

And what does "I did that" say about free will? (That's a whole other can of worms.)

I don't know.

What I do know is that The Experience was real to me and it was somehow intentional. It followed a well-worn script of good battling evil for the soul of a person as we see in many of our myths and stories. It was not random.

The Experience opened me up and made me more open to and less judgmental of those who claim these sorts of experiences. I feel I'm connected to something much, much bigger than I am. One with the universe and all that. I can feel it. So I'm watering it.

LETTER TO THE EDITOR

Some years ago I wrote a letter to the editor of the local newspaper regarding a story about one of the members of the House of Representatives here in Minnesota. The story talked about how she and her husband fasted and prayed for three days until God told her to run for office again. At the time I was appalled and wrote a snarky sort of letter wondering why the good lord didn't bother to tell Adolph Hitler to kill himself before exterminating millions, but did make certain to encourage the representative to go after another term.

We are at different ends of the political spectrum — she and I — and while I'm still not certain she heard God and therefore it might have been the wrong decision for her, I may be wrong. I'm in no position to know what did or did not happen to her, nor was I then. I know that now. I'm sorry, Ms. Bachman. We need to be able to disagree without being disparaging or disrespectful.

I will say I'm sorry for the song now also because eventually it will probably come out.

HOMOSUPERIORS

Everything is in a constant state of change, of evolution. And if God is everything, then evolution is God's way of living or modus operandi, which makes sense because evolution is fucking brilliant.

Contrary to other life on the planet, as far as we know, we are the only ones who consciously understand evolution, and we know that at a most basic level, our only real evolutionary mission here on this earth is to survive and propagate the species. I know it's not glamorous, but over time it's spectacular.

We're tasked with making certain we endure as a species, and in the meantime, improve upon ourselves, thereby passing our new and improved genes, knowledge and understanding on to the coming generations. And as a species that has discovered evolution and now understands how it works, we must.

That's it. That's our job. We work for The Evolution.

That means that children are our greatest asset and mission. It is always the next generation that will bring our species further into the future, and they need to be educated, groomed and prepared to do that – and better than us, way better – and they must do the same for the generation that follows them.

That's how we make a better world. That's where we affect the evolution of our species — the children. Education. Experience.

THAT BEING SAID

It is here then that I bestow upon new and future generations my wisdom and plead that they fix everything that we've fucked up. Remember the Peaceful Scientific Global Enlightenment bit from earlier in the book? That!

We are leaving you a world that is a colossal mess in so many ways. The generations that preceded you have created the biggest mass extinction since the dinosaurs, have killed off half of the natural world since 1970, some turn their backs to climate change rather than face it head on, and on and on. Our greed knows no bounds – we put profits over planet all the time. You all need to do the very opposite of much of what we've done.

Yeah, sorry about that.

Young people, despite our duties as adults to make sure each of you has the education and opportunities you deserve to do great things, we won't. We will probably cut our taxes first. When it comes to our military – "money is no object and we will invest in the best!" Education? "No sense in throwing all sorts of money at that." That's the way we think and why your education is horribly under-funded, you are racking up tens and hundreds of thousands of dollars in student loan debt, and why some of us like to actually blame the teachers themselves for the problems we've created.

But the real reason is that you are surrounded by anti-intellectuals – people who, for whatever reason, denigrate smart people, higher education, academics, experts and the like. Whether all that thinking overwhelms them, they're embarrassed because they don't understand it, or because it puts forth actual proof that conflicts with what they want to believe, they seem to want to be surrounded by stupid – and they want you to be stupid, too.

This has been going on for most of my adult life. Don't fall for it.

Public school is free, suck everything you can from it, but that is just the beginning. Seize your education as soon as you can understand this sentence and never let up. Challenge your mind and yourself constantly. In a big way, the more you know, the more you are, the more you have to work with, the more you see through bullshit. That's probably why they belittle smart people and like stupid so much. Smart people have well-founded opinions based on actual evidence and knowledge.

It's your pony to ride. Have at it. All the information is out there and accessible through our smart phones and free libraries. Take advantage of that or lose your advantage in the new world – wherever you are.

You've got one brain (that houses you) in a world where brains are in ascendance (and brawn increasingly useless). We continue to shed the jobs that don't require much brain work at a frenetic pace. Some are disappearing overseas, but most are going to automation, computers and robots. If you don't make yourself smart – really smart – you're going to be left behind. It doesn't matter if you're a city kid or country kid, suburbs or small town, the new world will demand your intellect and have little need for your biceps. Get smart or smart people are going to eat your lunch.

You know the saying, "There's no excuse for stupid"? There aren't going to be nearly as many jobs either.

Only you can make you smart. And only you can make you ignorant. We live. We learn. Always and constantly. Choose wisely and read widely. You have to be better than us – that's the whole point.

The mind is also the only place we can affect change with people who are ignorant and angry, people who hate, who kill and who are addicted. It is in the minds of ourselves and our children that we will improve the human race. And not until we understand and take control of our minds are we ever free from that which makes us suffer.

So when politicians denigrate science, make fun of academics or intellectuals, bureaucrats, career-this or that (also known as the people who actually know how complicated shit works and ultimately through whom the rest of us learn), stay smart and tell them to fuck off. You want smart on your side.

And if that's not enough to ponder (and with my father's final years in mind), know that according to The New York Times, studies suggest that higher learning creates more complicated connections between your nerve cells, which may help protect you against cognitive decline — dementia.[42]

WHAT DO I KNOW? WE ARE WHAT WE KNOW.

Knowledge is everything. We are the sum-total of our experiences, learning, memories and whatever genetic information was passed down from our two parents.

Understanding what we know for fact and what we just think we know is understanding ourselves; understanding our memories and how they evolve is understanding ourselves; understanding our emotional responses to the world is understanding ourselves; understanding why we are in error is understanding ourselves; understanding anything that is happening up there in our brains – our minds – is understanding ourselves. We reside there. Our brains are us.

Cravings, habits and addictions dominate much of our lives, our actions and the choices we make. Whatever we capture through our senses changes us – mostly imperceptibly, but sometimes profoundly. But like the unconscious mind dominates how our minds work, it's the imperceptible things, piling up over time, that dominate who we are.

I've learned that just watching some guy dangle from a skyscraper in a blockbuster movie can fire similar neurons in our own minds – so that we have an empathetic response that is similar and may even experience vertigo or piddle in our pants.

I've learned that a lot of us live a lot of our lives vicariously through fictional characters.

I learned that if we are willing to simply open up to the universe around us, we will see actual miracles right there in creation itself.

We make ourselves angry – most of the time.

I learned that spirituality is first and foremost a personal matter, like running. You can run with other people, but it's all your run.

It's been just a few generations since kids grew up with only the movie house to bask in the light of a screen. The world as they understood it, beyond what they read, was the world that unfolded right in front of them.

Only in the last couple of hundred years, in a million of years of human evolution, did our individual access to information go from pretty much nada for most of us to being able to access just about every piece of information in the entire world through the Internet and smart phones.

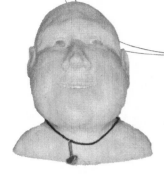

And through it all, and because of it all, I saw more clearly how important meditation is to the modern mind and science to the modern condition.

WHAT ELSE?

The modern world is also supremely interesting, complex, wondrous and beautiful. The modern mind even more so. And the modern malaise just needs some quiet meditation, more nature, wonder, focus and understanding, which will lead to more joy, balance and peace. Simple as that.

I'm certain that future generations – starting right now – can make different decisions and evolve the human race to be even more spectacular than we already are. Eradicate greed, encourage lovingkindness, help one another out. Remember also that the children of your father's enemies need not be your enemies. You can think – and act – differently in so many positive ways.

I also learned about Neuroplasticity – the malleable human mind. Neuroplasticity means we can, through the choices we make with repetition, experiences and emotions, make the mind we want to have in many ways. We've barely plumbed the depths of the human mind – as humanity and as individuals. We hardly even think about it. There are infinite opportunities to make our minds different, and better, at any age. And there is so much joy to be had in the process of learning, meditating and practicing anything. The mind can be shaped into whatever we can imagine – even as we age.

Our experiences shape us – for good and bad – and give us the arsenal of knowledge and ideas we each need to understand and conquer the world. Metaphorically. We don't need any more conquering, or killing, raping, stealing and all the rest – no matter what their religion, beliefs or life experiences.

IN THE END

Know your own mind, and admit what you know, what you just think you know, and what you don't know, then know and know and know some more. Use technology – and any other means – to expand your mind, but be careful expanding your mind; meditate, rid your life of useless anger, open up to the wonders of our stunningly beautiful and complex world and the boundless heavens all around us, and then just keep doing what you're doing.

When my father was still well, he told me that he wasn't afraid to die, but that he didn't want to miss anything after he was gone. I asked him if he believed there is a heaven, assuming I knew how the scientist in him would answer. Instead he said, "I don't know, but I sure hope so."

Me, too.

NOTES

[1] Lama Surya Das.

[2] Thich Nhat Hanh, "The Heart of the Buddha's Teaching: Transforming Suffering into Peace, Joy and Liberation," Parallax Press, 1998, p 9-11.

[3] Thich Nhat Hanh, p 78.

[4] Lewis, Marc, "The Biology of Desire: Why Addiction is Not a Disease," Public Affairs, 2015, p x.

[5] Marc Lewis, p 25

[6] Szalavitz, Maia, "Can You Get Over an Addiction?" The New York Times, June 26, 2016, p SR9.

[7] Marc Lewis, p 23.

8 Holland, Julie, "We medicate our moods and are the worse for it," SeattleTimes.com, October 8, 2015, http://www.seattletimes.com/opinion/we-medicate-our-moods-and-are-the-worse-for-it/.

9 Fleischman, Paul R., "Wonder: When and Why the World Appears Radiant," Small Batch Books, 2013, p 135.

10 Bowie, David, "Sound and Vision," Lodger.

11 Norton, Amy, "Limit Kids' Exposure to Media Violence, Pediatricians Say" Online Healthday.com, July 18, 2016, https://consumer.healthday.com/general-health-information-16/media-health-news-760/limit-kids-exposure-to-media-violence-pediatricians-say-712956.html

12 Thompson, Derek, "A World Without Work," The Atlantic, July/August 2015, p 55.

13 Thich Nhat Hanh, p 53.

14 Thich Nhat Hanh, p 52-53.

15 Dehaene, Stanislas, "Consciousness and the Brain: Deciphering How the Brain Codes Our Thoughts," Penguin Books, 2014, p 35-36.

16 Paul R. Fleischman, p 55.

17 Dobelli, Rolf. The Art of Thinking Clearly. Sceptre, 2013

[18] Swanbrow, Diane, "Empathy: College students don't have as much as they used to," Online: University of Michigan Institute for Social Research: University of Michigan News, May 27, 2010, http://ns.umich.edu/new/releases/7724-empathy-college-students-don-t-have-as-much-as-they-used-to.

[19] Mlodinow, Leonard, "Subliminal: How Your Unconscious Mine Rules Your Behavior," Vintage Books, 2013, p 194.

[20] Thich Nhat Hanh, p 51.

[21] The Buddha. Can't find original source. A little help?

[22] Phillips, Emo, live performance.

[23] Sacks, Oliver, "My Own Life: Oliver Sacks on Learning He Has Terminal Cancer," The New York Times, February 19, 2015, A25.

[24] "Beliefs about nicotine influence cigarette craving," Virginia Tech Carilion Research Institute, Online: http://research.vtc.vt.edu/news/2016/sep/13/beliefs-about-nicotine-influence-cigarette-craving/.

[25] Sides, John, "White Christian America is Dying," WashingtonPost.com, August 15, 2016, https://www.washingtonpost.com/news/monkey-cage/wp/2016/08/15/white-christian-america-is-dying/?utm_term=.f9a684818e22.

[26] Wilder, Thorton, "The Eighth Day," Harper, 1967.
27 Voltaire, Wit and Wisdom, The Week Magazine, June 2017.

[28] Yeats, W.B., Online: Poetseers.com, Nobel Prize Poets, William B Yeats, 1923,http://www.poetseers.org/nobel-prize-for-literature/william-b-yeats/Maclean's (Canada).

[29] Quammen, David, "Giant Sequoias," National Geographic, December 2012.

[30] Fleischman, p 102.

[31] Thich Nhat Hanh, "No Death, No Fear," Riverhead Books, 2002, p 34-35.

[32] Fleischman, p 191.

[33] Ananthaswamy, Anil, "Run Your Life on Autopilot," (part of) "The Other You: Six Things your Brain Can do when Your Back is Turned" New Scientist, October 1-7, 2016, p 34.

[34] Campbell, James. "Are We Raising a Generation of Nature-Phobic Kids?", Los Angeles Times Online, July 29, 2016. http://www.latimes.com/opinion/op-ed/la-oe-campbell-kids-fear-of-nature-20160729-snap-story.html.

[35] Williams, Florence. "This is Your Brain on Nature," National Geographic, January 2016, p 57.

[36] Williams, Florence.

[37] Williams, Florence.

[38] Pascal, Blaise, Online: TheWeek.com, September 30, 2016, http://theweek.com/print/790/46451/article

[39] Wildmind.org

[40] Eno, Brian, and Karl Hyde, "Slow Down, Sit Down, Breathe," High Life, 2014.

[41] "Mindfulness practice leads to increases in regional brain gray matter density," Hölzel, Britta K. et al., Psychiatry Research: Neuroimaging , Volume 191 , Issue 1 , 36 – 43.

[42] Belluck, Pam, "Education May Cut Dementia Risk, Study Finds," The New York Times, February 11, 2016, p A14.

[43] Prince, "I Wish U Heaven," Lovesexy, 1988.

SUGGESTED READING LIST

I also dedicate this book to these authors and their books, which I read while researching my own. I quote a little, but use a lot. I needed proof and these folks gave it to me.

Armstrong, Karen. A History of God: The 4,000 Year Quest of Judaism, Christianity and Islam. Alfred A. Knopf, Inc., 1993.

Beauregard, Mario, and O'Leary, Denyse. The Spiritual Brain: A Neuroscientists Case for the Existence of the Soul. Harper Collins Publishers, 2007.

Dehaene, Stanislas. Consciousness and the Brain: Deciphering How Our Brain Codes Our Thoughts. Penguin Books, 2014.

Dobelli, Rolf. The Art of Thinking Clearly. Sceptre, 2013.

Fleischman, MD., Paul, R. Wonder: When and Why the World Appears Radiant. Sceptre, 2013.

Hanh, Thich Nhat. The Heart of the Buddha's Teaching: Transforming Suffering into Peace, Joy and Liberation. Small Batch Books, 2013.

Hanh, Thich Nhat. The Art of Power. Broadway Books, 1999.

Hanh, Thich Nhat. The Miracle of Mindfulness. Beacon Press, 1975.

Lewis, Marc. The Biology of Desire: Why Addiction is Not a Disease. Harper Collins, 2007.

Mlodinow, Leonard. Subliminal: How Your Unconscious Mind Rules Your Behavior. Beacon Press, 1975.

Sacks, Oliver. Hallucinations. Public Affairs, 2015.

Wildmind Buddhist Meditation. www.wildmind.org

ACKNOWLEDGEMENTS

Behind every man: I thank my wife, Jana, for your intelligence, love, support and assistance. You made room for me to create this and I love you for it!

I thank my great parents, Bob and Mimi, for being great parents. That's the bottom line, right there.

My sister, Kristin, and brothers, Daniel and Jonathan, for their love and support (and for allowing me to be such a great brother to them).

Dave and Pat, because you're always there for me.

Christina LeClaire, for graphic design, and everyone else at Mod for support and all around coolness.

Lynn Bronson, for an early review and some much needed encouraging words.

Debbie Kuehn, for editing, kind words and friendship. (Any errors that remain are my own.)

The rest of my extended family and to all the teachers of the world. You are on the front line in the battle against stupid. I thank you for your service.

68544163R00118

Made in the USA
Lexington, KY
13 October 2017